Tempting Letters:
Letters from an experienced demon to a novice

B. Koppany III

STRIKING IMPRESSIONS
Hawthorne, California
1995

Copyright © 1992, 1995 by B. Koppany III

All rights reserved under International and Pan-American Copyright Conventions. Published in the United States by

STRIKING IMPRESSIONS
P.O. Box 926 Hawthorne, CA   USA   90251-0926
(310) 644-6796

Library of Congress Cataloging-in-Publication Data

Koppany, B.
Tempting Letters: Letters from an experienced demon to a novice / by
B. Koppany III.
p. cm.
ISBN 0-9639422-1-2
1. Christian life--Fiction. 2. Temptation--Fiction. 3. Christian ethics--
Fiction. I. Title.
BV4515.2.K66 1995   248.4

Library of Congress Catalog Card Number 95-68354

Printed in the United States of America
by Griffin Printers, Glendale, California

First Edition

My dear Christian Brother and Sister,

I suppose this all began with a radio sermon by Chuck Swindoll on June 1, 1990. It was about the devil. I scurried to reread *The Screwtape Letters* by C. S. Lewis as a response.

These letters are timeless. They were written by C. S. Lewis and ended at World War II, but people 50 years later have to face new challenges in their spiritual journey. The problems of the world have changed. Today the family unit has fallen out of grace. The divorce rate is higher than 50 percent. Single-parent families are the rule and not the exception. Abortion is legalized. Drugs are prevalent and even touted in our culture. Church attendance is alarmingly low.

I do not flatter myself that I am C. S. Lewis, but it has been a challenge for me to write *Tempting Letters* for the 1990's. In contact with the C. S. Lewis estate, they said that I may state that my book was inspired by *The Screwtape Letters*.

I want to acknowledge Reverend Earl Palmer, who was then at the Berkeley First Presbyterian Church, who introduced me, and the entire congregation, to C. S. Lewis. Especially, I would like to thank Reverend Jack Buckley, also at Berkeley First Presbyterian Church, who was there while I was discovering C. S. Lewis, and who has been a prayer partner with me for years. Also appreciated is Reverend Ron White, Jr., who gave me some needed pointers on the first draft of this project. A special dedication goes to Professor Daniel P. Fuller, Professor Mitties DeChamplain, Charles M. Schulz, and Dr. David Hocking, the finest Christian instructors I've ever had. My thanks go to Ms. Belinda Smith, a wonderful woman who did a superb job of transcribing my dictations. Ms. Laura Zehnder did the initial editing—Thanks, Laura. Mr. Jim Shea did the second editing—Thanks, Jim.

I felt a calling and perceived a need to write letters of my own. A big reason for the calling for me to write this manuscript is that it came at the end of my first year in the seminary. I was having trouble dealing with people who were academicians first, thinking with their minds, and Christians second, thinking with their hearts. These people seemed to lack the love and joy of Christ.

I feel it is good not to dwell on this book too much. I never realized how wonderfully precious the words "God" and "Christ" sounded to my ears. I have had to forego them in this text by using the words "Enemy" and "Son"...I've missed the words "God" and "Christ" so much in my life while doing this project.

An eternal dedication goes to my wonderful wife, Margi, who radiates the Christian walk for the world to see. I delight in her and use her constantly as an example for me.

I hope you enjoy this and see the love and face of Christ in it, for this is a love offering of me to Him. I look forward to you joining me in this adventure. Welcome.

Sincerely yours in Christ,

B. Koppany III

Tempting Letters:

Letters from an experienced demon to a novice

Letter Number One

My dear nephew Bieshorn,

These are wonderful days we are living in right now. People, the grotesque fleshly beings that they are, are turning themselves over to us without our raising a paw or fighting, thanks to Our Father Below. Since their second World War, we have been extremely busy down here.

First, we have destroyed the family unit. Although this has not been easy to accomplish, it has been worthwhile and has born much fruit. Mothers and fathers fight. Divorce is at an all time high, and there is more child abuse than ever. Praise Our Father Below. We have increased sexual desires in humans and twisted the sexual act, raising it to a plateau never seen before. Drugs have been increased, with a higher percentage of the population taking them.

Besides the above, we have been actively involved in increasing church problems. Churches are dividing left and right over petty issues. Those scandals with televangelism were great public relations for our cause, weren't they? Membership is now at an all-time low. These certainly are great days for us.

People, at least the ones these days, want something they can see with their eyes and touch with their hands. Have you noticed how some of these people are calling other people crazy who believe in things unseen, i.e., the Enemy? We have been working ever so hard at this, and you can see how good we've been at obtaining this slanted viewpoint. From your tempting lessons, you know you're either the "eator" or the "eatee" in Hell. Our slowness to act is the fastest way to a quick demise in Our Father Below's house. Thankfully, here in Hell there is always someone who is quite willing to step over or on you, as the case may be, given the least provocation.

The Enemy, confound Him and His pathway, is very difficult to outfox, even for us. His is a pathway of things unseen. Humans have not realized the fact that they all have many chances to see the Enemy's hideously lit path. We do know that if they do not follow the Enemy by the time their souls depart from the lump of flesh they are contained in, they are ours by default. Praise Our Father Below.

We have noticed recently in the last few decades that the big "sinners" have been decreasing. There aren't the admirable Hitlers or Eichmanns of the good old days. One of the problems with this is that men and women have been losing their individuality as the world shrinks. This can be good for our cause. Humans with blinders on are following others like lambs led by following a bell to the slaughter. Have you noticed how cults are on an increase?

This has not been all due to our efforts, but we will take the credit. We have discovered that if we let these sheep wander, they typically will not find the Enemy's narrow gate by themselves. The Enemy has to help somehow. Left to themselves, they will naturally wander their way to Our Father Below. With time, it has been getting easier and easier to reel these humans in. They are jumping into our boat before we can bait our hooks!

Now, getting down to business, to my understanding you have just been assigned a new patient. He is a young man in his 20's, nothing spectacular about him, but that is not the important point. The point is that he comes to us one way or another. I do see by his dossier that your patient is out of school and working. That is good. Keep him occupied.

It is important for him to be busy! Keep him busy with his job, with parties, and devise ways to occupy his time as much as you can. Be devious. We're good at that.

It is important not to let your patient be "happy." We should keep him itching for something he will not find and looking for something unworthy to ceaselessly search for. He should be following searchlights at night to end up at a used car lot instead of finding the rainbow he is looking for.

It is important not to let your patient plant his feet firmly on the ground. We have to keep him moving. If he does plant his feet, he might stand still long enough to see a direction to move in. That direction can be deadly to our cause. The longer he looks down and not up toward the Enemy, the harder it is for him to look up. Humans are creatures of habit. If he keeps looking down, sooner or later, he will head in that direction straight to us.

I have noted in the dossier that your patient does not want to be different and does not want to rock the boat. That is wonderful. He should let others determine his priorities—preferably us. He will probably follow us as well as someone else, and hopefully end up being led around by those who follow us already.

Your patient, as I have seen from reviewing his file, looks to me to be an easy victory. He has had extremely limited exposure to the Enemy. If we do not make a mistake, he is sure to be ours. I will write you more about assuring this success in days to come, but keep your eye open and be aware. Do not give your patient a chance to let the Enemy in.

Affectionately yours.

Your uncle,

Korizo

Letter Number Two

My dear nephew Bieshorn,

I was disappointed, very disappointed indeed, to hear that the patient is a nominal Christian. I have found out through my own sources that the patient is even going to church occasionally. Isn't that a revolting thought? Church! Church can be very harmful. This was "forgotten" in your initial assessment of the patient. I can assure you that there will be serious repercussions if you are "forgetful" again in the future.

I see from my sources that the patient did enjoy Sunday School teachers when he was young. Although keeping him out of religious schools was difficult, a good job was done by that demon, your predecessor, who has moved up the eternal ladder to fry bigger fish. It will be to our benefit in the long run with the little religious training he had.

We have to minimize any time he spends near the Enemy on Sunday. Have the patient "party" until late Saturday night, then feel guilty on Sunday, but not go to church because he is too tired or sick to go. Have the patient too tired from his Saturday night fever, not set his alarm clock, not want to dress up for church or, better yet, have other "more important" things to do.

Have the patient flipping television stations on Sunday morning if he is able to get out of bed. Have the television evangelists generally talk down to him, shouting at him that he is damned and will die eternally. Patients seem to loathe that, which is good for our cause. Be sure the television shows say that the only true joy in life is to send in money at the end of the show.

Entice him to turn on shopping channels on television. Those are good for nothing and will further waste the patient's time. If that fails, have the patient see people shouting at him loudly on street corners about being damned. Try to make these people seem as fanatical as they can be!

It is amazing how many nominal Christians visit the Enemy or think about Him only on Sunday morning and, thankfully, most people these days do not think about the Enemy at all. Praise Our Father Below.

One of the most wonderful ways to praise Our Father Below on Sunday is to wash the car. Car washing is a good way to waste time and not draw the patient nearer to the Enemy. Other ways to draw the patient from the Enemy include going to flea markets and looking for a bargain. Let us not forget, one of the greatest ways for the patient to never think of the Enemy at all is general puttering around the house. There is ALWAYS something that needs to be done at home.

If the patient is like most people, he will not have money to spend on church. Giving money to the Enemy is the last priority on his list. Have him think of the collection plate as a deterrent to going to church. Let him think that the people surrounding him will scornfully look at him trying to pass the plate along without putting anything in it. The patient will assume that these people only want his money. He obviously does not realize that the money is going to be used for the Enemy's work. And, as you know too well, Bieshorn, this is definitely the only "good" endeavor that the patient can ever use his money on.

It is important for the patient to think of spiritual things as boring and no fun. Sermons in church are going to be long and tedious. Parking is going to be a burden and a chore. He will be seated in a position in church where he cannot see anyone, especially the pastor. He might even have to sit next to someone he would never think of associating with during the week. I expect our patient will want to sleep during the sermon because of being tired from Saturday night's efforts.

While sitting in church, have the patient concentrate his puny mind on the material objects in the world as much as he can. Items that he wants to purchase, accumulating a fat bank account, and the like are good ways to keep him occupied.

Oh, by the way, I noticed that the patient is in debt. That is a very good sign. The patient should be trained so that he is thinking about what other people have and what he lacks.

We should try our hardest to make sure that every holiday is turned into material events. Always play down the spiritual side of things. We should try to make sure that Thanksgiving is to celebrate the start of Christmas shopping. We should think of Christmas as being an excuse to exchange and get gifts, and not to praise the birth of the Enemy's Son. Easter can be used as the last chance to go skiing before the season is over and summer starts. Should you need more help on this, please consult your tempter's handbook for other ideas.

It is important that the spiritual world (the Enemy and Enemy's world) should be compared to the "real" material world. Use the "real" world as the standard, not the other way around. For example, have the patient notice how business buildings are taller and more beautiful than churches, which are miniscule and pitiful in comparison. This will subconsciously support our position on the importance of "reality" over "spirituality." It is important that the patient should not be grateful for what he has, but make sure that he only thinks of what he lacks. For if he is grateful, he will think about who he is being grateful to. We have to keep his eyes moving. We always have to give him something to do to keep his mind off the Enemy.

I have noticed that he is over his head with work to do at the office. This is a very good sign. Keep him concentrating on Administrivia. Most bipeds usually do not ask themselves questions that are bigger than themselves. Especially when they don't have easy answers. They only ask questions they themselves can answer. It is important not to let your patient look up to the stars. We never want him to see greatness on a scale that is beyond his mind to comprehend. Do try to assure he never looks beyond the reach of his arm for anything.

And above all, never show the patient true beauty. For beauty always highlights the difference between the material and the spiritual. We do not want him to look inside and ask himself questions such as: Am I happy? Am I complete? What is lacking in my life?

Remember from your lessons that the Enemy is different from us in many ways. The Enemy is not cruel; He is just. Remember that we must tip the balance scales towards our side. Incredibly small victories will win the war.

I hope to hear better things very soon about the patient's disturbing habit of going to church. Remember, if we do not get great achievements from you, you will not get another chance to achieve anything, great or small.

Affectionately yours,

Your uncle,

Korizo

Tempting Letters

Letter Number Three

My dear nephew Bieshorn,

I have noticed that your patient is trying very hard to please other people. While this can be devastating, it certainly is not a problem here. It is obvious that your patient wants desperately to belong to a group. He wants to look up to others and be looked up to by others. This is a worldly trait that we have encouraged and is not relevant at all to the Enemy or His wishes. When your patient tries to please others this way, he takes his mind off the Enemy.

Your patient is getting dangerously close to the Enemy when he finds out that most of what he can see and touch is just a facade. Your patient should concentrate on purchasing material objects: stereos, cameras, fancy doodads, watches and other things that have absolutely no meaning in life. We have to keep your patient from doing important things with his mind and channel his mind so he worships materialism.

Encourage your patient to buy what he is missing in life. Make your patient feel it is his birthright to do so. Remember, always give your patient options in his purchases. The more options your patient has, the more time he will waste considering them. This way your patient will not think at all about the Enemy or notice the Enemy's presence inside and outside of his being.

Your patient should always equate instant gratification with true happiness. He should not realize that the Enemy's plan is to comfort the afflicted and afflict the comfortable.

It is important to try to make your patient want to be something or someone other than himself. When people strive to be individuals, the more they strive, the more they achieve mediocrity and conformity. Superficial methods such as cosmetic surgery, makeup, clothing, working out, will provide the necessary distractions. Anything to change a human's body is beneficial! For example, I'm sure you know that eye surgeries can let people see without glasses. They can change their eye color with contact lenses. We want people to use just about anything to show that the eye is more important than the soul, not just the window to it. And if they want to look inside, we have developed psychological sciences to confuse them even more.

It is also important that your patient never catches up with his peers. Always keep him behind. We want your patient never to catch his breath. Keep him on the tread-mill! It is very enjoyable watching humans sweat in their race after vapors that are not worth the chase in the first place.

By their striving for an idealized beauty, we have twisted this culture. Magazines about movie stars and "beautiful people" are great. Inundate your patient every way possible. Have beautiful people on television, in newspapers and magazines, and on the radio. Use beautiful people for everything from selling car parts to cockroach sprays. Have your patient value their opinions based on their beauty alone.

Your patient should change lifestyles as frequently as people change hairstyles. One of Our Father Below's best tricks is to have your patient on a constant battle with his weight—called dieting. Diets are wonderful ways to keep your patient constantly miserable. Since gluttony and over-indulgence are enviable traits to have, he will actually look forward to his death-move down below. He will soon be lost to the Enemy, and become ours. If your patient rebels, slide him into a group that is ostracized from the community.

Lust abounds these days! Just the sound of the word "lust" give my throat a lovely regurgitating feeling to it. Everyone is lusting after everyone else and sex has become a bargaining chip. It gratifies me that people are thinking with their eyes and glands but not with their minds. I am glad that the Enemy gave us sex so that we can pervert it. Sex these days can now be graded on a scale. Happily, it cannot be graded on an absolute level because there is always someone new showing up to compare with.

Comparing one person to another will not let your patient find true contentment. These seeds of discord sown by comparisons will grow into large, thick walls, making relationships impossible to maintain. It is through our long and hard work that the divorce rate has steadily raised and is now greater than 50 percent. However, we do have orders from the eternal police to make the goal of divorce 100 percent in the near future. We are working hard toward that. We have to destroy the family to obtain ultimate success!

The world tolerates everything these days. There are no rules or discretions. The adage "let it all hang out" (devised by one of our publicists), says it all.

In closing, I am slightly disappointed to find out that your patient is still going to church. Try to see if you can do something productive about that. I look forward to hearing from you with more news of your achievement.

Affectionately yours,

Your uncle,

Korizo

Letter Number Four

My dear nephew Bieshorn,

I read that our patient is very unhappy and feeling inadequate because of the chaos that is surrounding him. This is excellent news.

Our patient has forgotten that the Enemy made humans to depend upon Him. They are inadequate by design. Humans are less than what they can be and should be. The Enemy freely gives them power and strength to do anything. When fleshly beings breathe, eat, think, and act, it is a gift from Him (like the Enemy's Son). Why couldn't the Enemy give humans something useless like tasteless kitchen serving dishes they are so fond of giving each other? After all, that is what humans give to others they love, isn't it? Why give them a human/deity to show them how He wants them to live? One of our hardest tasks is continually recreating religious decoys!

Our patient should not try to do the Enemy's works by imitating the Enemy's Son. If our patient avoids recognition and admiration, he is clearly acting for the Enemy. I read that he calls his parents to find out how they are. We must stop this! Without realizing it, his every unselfish act is definitely geared towards following the Enemy.

Thankfully, our patient does not realize that the Enemy gives gifts to people in different ways. We are pleased to see that some people feel inadequate with their gifts. It is amazing to us that the cursed Enemy blesses everyone one way or another. I don't understand how the Enemy can give something without expecting an equal return! Why is the Enemy so magnanimous? It is a mystery to me. He must be up to something. Curse Him!

The Enemy thinks small things are as important as large things. Every time our patient helps someone, or even smiles at someone, he unselfishly glorifies the Enemy. Our Father Below does not understand this. The Enemy says our patient is perfected in weakness. Our Father Below's power is perfected in strength. We have learned that strength wins over weakness, fair fight or not.

Remember our problems with Peter? He denied the Son time and time again! But, sadly, the Enemy grabbed Peter and hung onto him tenaciously, much to our dismay. Peter smelled too much like the Enemy after that for us to get close and grab a good hold no matter what we tried. Remember this lesson that I learned centuries ago; if our patient fails, it is good for us. However, if our patient fails too much of the time, the Enemy usually grabs him.

It is relatively easy to make our patient feel he is incapable of great things. Give him small successes like winning a game of Trivial Pursuit. This is one of our greatest inventions! Some patients even play Biblical Trivial

Pursuit. This keeps our patient's mind further off the Enemy and glued to trivialities. This twist of using the Enemy's words against him is one of our greatest ironies. The Enemy would hate things like this, but the Enemy is beyond such pettiness....so we hear.

Try to impede our patient from seriously beginning anything. Remember that small accidents always stop big actions. Make a pen run out of ink; provide a flat tire on the car; make sure there is no paper to write with; or even throw our patient a crossword puzzle or a newspaper. Do anything to keep him occupied! If he is constantly busy, he'll never have time to think of the Enemy and glorify Him. When your creativity fails you, you can always send our patient to the bathroom to occupy his time with normal human functions.

Remember, we have taught you that hideously beautiful paintings all start with one brush stroke. Even great books that glorify the Enemy were formed letter by letter. Get our patient to do things for recognition, admiration or money; not the Enemy.

The universe almost belongs to Our Father Below. Every effort for Our Father Below works for His final goal. Every effort against Him works for Him when we turn it around.

By the way, is our patient still going to church? Did you omit this deliberately? We are not sure. We have ways of finding out. I expect an answer to this forthcoming.

Affectionately yours,

Your uncle,

Korizo

Letter Number Five

My dear nephew Bieshorn,

Your patient what? Became more than a nominal Christian? Somehow, somewhere, you lowered your devilish guard! The Enemy snuck in and grabbed him! He waltzed in right under your noses. Your patient instantly knew that only the Enemy could remove the ache inside of him. Your patient realized that he was missing a piece of his soul! I can't believe that! Your patient even accepted the Son as Lord??! My stomachs churn at the prospect! How could you let this happen?

Let us hope, and hope very much, in the power of Our Father Below. I "pray" that your patient does not start reading the Bible seriously. We have found that if he seeks the Enemy, he will find the Enemy. If your patient asks anything ever so slowly or softly from the Enemy to glorify Him, the Enemy will respond.

You are in deep, deep trouble! If this mortal gets away, you won't escape us. Although it looks bleak, things could be worse. We must take action immediately!

Since your patient is now a Christian in more than name, he will probably start reading the Bible. They all do. Try to get your patient a Bible that paraphrases or interprets constantly! Find a copy that dilutes and warps the Enemy's words. There are many of these around.

I noted that you said your patient is smiling more often. That is very bad. Oh no! I see that your patient has even been baptized!!! Heavens! I just said the "B" word! I'm turning into a hairy wart. Now, Snaiglime, my assistant, has to finish writing this for me. I won't have any hands.

(A new hand takes over the writing)

We are still trying to figure out the "B" word. Our scientists have been working on this for centuries. We think, though we are not exactly sure, that your patient is sprinkled, immersed, or dunked with plain water. Nothing more. Just plain water. Somehow, it turns your patient into a new creation. We have to treat the creature differently now. Do not forget that our patient can now fight us!

With the "B"-tism your patient swears allegiance to the Enemy. It is now a formal declaration of war. All kid gloves are off. It should be noted that your patient is now armed with an arsenal, although a limited one. His new weapons include truth, righteousness, the Gospel, faith, salvation, and the Holy Spirit. These "limited" means are at his disposal. He can call upon them to defend himself and attack us at any time.

Once your patient is watered with that accursed solution, he is like an appealing caterpillar that has died and become one of those ugly butter-fluttering, flying things. Since your patient has committed himself we have to attack him more frequently!

I surely hope that you did whatever you could to make the "B"-tism occur quickly. Hopefully, it was over fast and not very memorable. Regrettably, I have noticed that most patients do remember their "B"-tism all of their lives. I would be very interested to find out what feeble attempts you made to stop the "B"-tism.

Perhaps one of the most crippling weapons you could have used was the mosquito. How the Enemy erred and created this wonderful proponent to our cause is unknown, but we have taken full advantage of His mistake neverthe-less. You could have used its needle-like proboscis to jar your patient's mind and body off the Enemy during this infamous event. When used sparingly, the mosquito could condition your patient to head in whatever direction we choose. I'm disappointed that you haven't used it yet. It was clearly stated in your tempting guide under the heading of "Petty Annoyances." Don't you remember the tempter's poem we drilled into you? As it does take nine hours to recite the entire poem, the pertinent part of it is:

"....And up in the air the mosquito is there. And what is more lewd...some bugs in the food."

I am sure that you will observe that your patient will not respond to you and your efforts the same as he has in the past. Try to keep your patient from looking for the Enemy. If he does, he will see the Enemy's hand in everything. Be optimistic towards your patient's outcome although you don't deserve it. Our Father Below knows full well that even those closer to the Enemy than your patient can stray. It makes them that much tastier to us.

Praise His Lowness for understanding feeble evangelists. These delectable worms' attempts at inept conversions (as your patient may hopefully turn out to be) get us 50 new converts to our cause. These evangelizing people on street corners, although not guided by us, are wonderful proponents for our cause. They turn patients towards our camp quicker than they would normally get there on their own steam. New Christians have a charmingly condescending attitude, condemning everyone who is different from them. We can use their pride to direct people to us quicker.

Now that he knows what the Enemy is offering him, your patient is brighter and harder to get at. You are going to have to work harder and be more cunning. Your performance has been lackluster thus far. Although your tempter's handbook pales compared to my priceless advice, I hope you have not thrown it out yet.

You should try to get at the small seed that the Enemy has planted inside your patient. Make sure it will not grow! If it does, chances are that it will bring up others. We cannot afford this!

I expect to hear better news from you soon.

Affectionately yours,

Your uncle,

Korizo (via Snaiglime)

Tempting Letters

Letter Number Six

My dear nephew Bieshorn,

Having commanded an underling, Grulsnort, the tedious task of checking our archives, I found out to date, that no tempter has reversed a "B"-tism. Reversing a "B"-tism is an impossibility; we think. Can't you do anything to keep our patient from reading the Bible? I also know he is attending church services. If two are gathered in the Enemy's cursed name, He is definitely there. As we know all too well, we literally cannot stand near the presence of the Enemy. It is too painful!

We know that the change in u patient after a "B"-tism is not a permanent one. People who have been "B"-tized can still come to our camp. I suggest you use our time-proven strategy on our patient that the Enemy does not want or cannot use material possessions. Create the illusion for our patient that the Enemy and His material world are separate.

Make sure our patient cannot find the section in the Bible on how the Enemy feeds crows who lack possessions. (No, I don't know where the section is.) We know the Enemy will take care of people who are more valuable to Him than crows. Let our patient dwell more on the gifts than on the giver of the gifts. Have our patient give himself material "rewards" for small successes, defeats, and failures. Have the patient purchase the latest cassette or videotape, so that he may see things over and over again. Things like this are wonderful time wasters and a sign of our ingenuity.

I am still pleased to see that you are pulling whatever strings we have attached to our patient's soul, luring him and dragging him along towards our camp. When I see our patient's lust for material things, this encourages me. Convince him that the Enemy will provide for his wants as well as his needs, then disappoint him! Convince the patient that lusting for "things" is normal. Everyone wants "stuff." Isn't "stuff" a pretty sounding word? It almost sounds like a barking dog or some delightful curse.

Never let the lust for material objects disappear. It is important for our patient to consider variety the "spice" of life. Have this lusting desire change into a different item, or even better, items. Always keep things varied. The more our patient spends on materialistic objects the less time he will concentrate on his spiritual well-being. He will spend less time praying. I assume your patient is praying and talking to the Enemy regularly. Disgusting!

Do not forget to vary materialistic goals. This is important! Always change these goals so that their acquisition is an end in itself.

Find him an idol to emulate. Make it someone he will want to compete with. Keep our patient playing catch-up with this human-made goal by holding him back. But never hold him behind for long or he may want to give up competing. If our patient is never satisfied, gluttony could be one of the sins we can reel him in with later on.

Try to get our patient to spend time on a vapid, time-consuming project. Have him make a clock or a shower-curtain rod, anything that will "save" money for other materialistic treats. But never give our patient a true feeling of accomplishment. You can always concentrate on the flaw in the project.

Use music as a distraction when you can, but this is a double-edged sword. Music, remember, can help bring our patient to the Enemy or show him beauty. Beauty "evolves" from the Enemy. But most music today, praise Our Father Below, is noise. Anyone can easily notice that the lyrics were definitely written by proponents of our cause. Frankly, our efforts have developed to the point that we don't even try to hide our presence in the music anymore. Try not to let our patient think about the devilishly evil lyrics. Have him repeat lyrics subconsciously throughout the day. This is a wonderful way for our patient to constantly praise Our Father Below.

Praise to Our Father Below and do not let yourself relax for an instant. We are watching you.

Affectionately, more or less,

Your uncle,

Korizo

P.S. Oh, yes, I am back to normal once again, although being a wart does have certain advantages in our profession.

Letter Number Seven

My dear nephew Bieshorn,

I see from your last letter that your patient just met a woman at a party. Parties are some of the best places for our strongest efforts against the Enemy. It is peer pressure that does our work for us. Parties are very good places for your patient to meet the opposite sex. Not as good as a bar or pub, but not bad.

Reading a little further, I am a bit disappointed to see he did not use any pickup lines that have sexual connotations. No, "Your place or mine?," "You'd look great in a swimsuit!" or "Don't say a thing; just let me look at you." Try to instill the "normal" male gender in your patient. From what I have observed, I can see signs of puppy love rearing its ugly head. I can envision him and the young lady smiling at each other in a horribly attractive way. I imagine it was probably their smiles that brought them together.

Distract them with lust. This is always a great weapon between the sexes. Never let them communicate about "real" things. Keep their relationship extremely superficial. They should ask non-spiritual questions to each other. I can hear it now: "Where would you like to eat?"..."What do you think of fashions, or TV shows?"..."How about a game of bridge?" This mindless chatter is music to my ear.

Have him try to impress her with his "stuff." Have her try to impress him with her "stuff." Make it a competition! His "stuff" and her "stuff," or vice versa. Have them compare each other to people they know. Old boyfriends and girlfriends are always good for mental anguish. When he tries to impress her, have him take her somewhere expensive. Any place way beyond his means. Extravagance always produces good returns for us down the road.

Oh no! I just read that she is a Christian, too! Curse it!! This is not going well at all. I can sense the Enemy's hideous hand in this. Don't let the lovebirds anywhere near churches, religious events, or church socials!

On the positive side, I read that you checked her dossier and I am relieved to see that she is not too despicable to us. This is good. I would suggest having the eternal police review her statistics for strikes against her. Does she follow the Enemy well? Is she worldly?

Reveal each other's annoying habits. Things that are peevish stew and stir within their minds. Make these annoying habits grow over time. For example: he spits a lot, she chews gum...things like that. You have been taught these little habits lurking within them. If not, you can always consult your tempter's guide for the standard list of "teeth-gnashing foibles," or use your fiendish imagination.

Create obvious disparities between them. Good ones include social and financial differences. Make it seem like they are the princess and the toad. Show them they are worlds apart. However, if they are truly miserable being around each other, then have them develop a strong relationship, for they deserve each other. This effort in laying a strong foundation of misery will yield some wonderful despair in the future harvest.

On second thought, maybe they are social drinkers and you could use that to break apart a possibly dangerous relationship with the Enemy. As I'm sure you know from your history, sometimes the Enemy merges two followers into one flesh and makes them much stronger followers. As you wrote, they sadly are both Christians. This is something we have to be on our guard against at all times. Try to keep them noisy and busy with each other if you can't separate them from the Enemy. Remember, the Enemy created the world with just a word. But He talks to people in whispers, and it has to be quiet for them to hear Him.

Whatever you do, don't send them out to a movie that has social or ethical themes. This will make them ask worldly questions and answer them with moral answers that may involve spirituality. This is deadly to us! What if they agree on these issues?

These two people may have servant mentalities. Make each one imagine that the other is their ideal mate. This way, everything will become magnified and out of proportion. This will help make it more difficult to please each other.

Now, I can definitely see the Enemy's hand in this. He is omnipresent and I knew He would catch up with things, sooner or later. You clearly must have been asleep to let him sneak by, but we both know that demons can't sleep! If you'd like, I could assign a minor devil to prod you with a pitchfork whenever you deviate from your task. Let me know if you are interested in this.

Christianity could very well be a common bond for these two. This is a problem. Even if these fleshy lumps try to follow the Enemy, following is almost the same as success. The Enemy knows it is important that your patient follows Him. He wants your patient to follow Him, whether or not your patient succeeds. The Enemy will forgive him independent of our efforts to trip or divert him from the narrow pathway he's on.

Thankfully, your patient may never realize that the narrow path goes along a sheer cliff that we will gleefully push him from when the situation presents itself. Don't relax your vigil! Never give up! This may be the last "friendly" warning you'll hear from me.

Maybe this possible girlfriend thing will keep your patient out of church. If he is busy spending time with her it might keep him from reading the Bible. Let us hope so.

Work the situation to your advantage. I hope to hear better things in the future.

Affectionately yours,

Your uncle,

Korizo

Tempting Letters

Letter Number Eight

My dear nephew Bieshorn,

I see from your latest letter that our patient thinks himself an extremely good catch because he appeals to a woman. This is very good news! Play upon his vanity.

I'm certain our patient feels his appeal is because of his intellect. Deep inside he knows it is the only thing he has going for him. I was pleased to see that our patient is unknowingly using his intellect to slowly turn the girl's affection away from him. This is a good trend. Knowledge enables our patient to exalt himself. Have him build on this foundation to make him believe he is superior to everyone.

I think our patient is basically a know-it-all. If he does not know, he will probably lie and say he does. Have our patient use his "valued" knowledge to draw conclusions based on his infinitesimal knowledge base. Even though his knowledge may turn out to be true and not merely conjecture, knowledge, as we all know, puffs up patients.

Try to make our patient a "Pharisee." He is right and never wrong and it's his way or nothing at all. Do everything in your power to make him think he's one rung beneath the cursed Trinity and at least one rung above everyone else. This will prove very much to our advantage when he is trying to relate to others.

Have our patient use his intellect by explaining everything. Blind him with his knowledge so he won't glimpse the Enemy's hand in the world around him. Try to assure that our patient does not see his blatantly obvious limitations. Give our patient an ego to counteract the wisdom the Enemy has given him.

The lies our patient tells will make him stumble over himself. The Enemy's wisdom makes fools of intellectuals. However, patients will try to explain everything, usually based on their own meager viewpoints. Try to get our patient to bask in his own knowledge. He will become dependent upon himself and not upon the Enemy.

Give our patient some small advance at work. Then, give him much more work and fewer dollars than it is worth. This will make our patient angry because he thinks he deserves more. At the same time, it will make him proud because he knows how good he really is. Try to have others put him on a pedestal that he does not have to descend from. And, to accomplish this, it is always best to have others lie to him. Have our patient feel that people cannot survive without him. Puff his ego up.

Once significantly loaded with ego and puffed up, our patient will quietly, without a whimper, roll into our camp and onto our tables. I apologize for the brevity of this, but we have been "advised" to attend a mandatory lecture on the nuances of subtle obnoxious tempting. I want to arrive early so I won't have to expend any energy by ousting a subordinate demon out of my uncomfortable seat.

Affectionately yours,

Your uncle,

Korizo

Tempting Letters

Letter Number Nine

My dear nephew Bieshorn,

I thought it an interesting question in your last letter when you asked what to do about his girlfriend. I assume his female acquaintance is now elevated to the status of a "girlfriend?" Is your question, "What should I do when she asks him to go to church?" We're talking about church and not their relating to each other, aren't we?

My opinion is that any church anyone goes to is bad. However, it is always worse for them and better for us if they go to someone else's church rather than their usual place of worship. We can easily show your patient that he and his girlfriend are not compatible because of religious differences. Make them see that each other's religious service professes to be superior. This develops an enchanting bias against going to other church services. Your patient will not realize that there are many ways to worship the Enemy. The Enemy is overjoyed at what little He receives in prayers. We, however, want it all.

Make denomination differences bigger. Provoke someone in church to make a blatant claim that they are the "true" church. Make them believe that everyone else is inferior. Keep the parishioners away from any true "soul" food. The Enemy has little room for judgmental people with Him in heaven. We think, however, they give a certain "flavor" to things down here.

Make small changes in church that will disturb and annoy your patient. Place Bibles with small print in the church. You can change the word "Mass" to "Holy Communion" or "Eucharist." This will annoy your patient like an itch he cannot scratch.

The "Our Father" prayer, as you know, was stolen from us. Even though modified for the Enemy's glory, we can use this prayer against your patient. For example, change the word "trespasses" to "debts." This will eventually make your patient question everything within the religious world. Take communion, for example. Some churches use wine and some use grape juice. Some churches have communion every six weeks while others have communion daily. Confuse him by exposing him to all types of communion. Always keep him guessing! Use big words if you have to! Words like "transubstantiation" of the host will get him so confused, he won't know which way is up!

Some churches will exclude people unless they believe exactly what their church says. These churches ultimately play homage to Our Father Below by their skewed priorities and consequent actions toward their fellow humans. These select churches are more effective, in my esteem, than having an out-and-out witch coven or cult to draw patients into.

Try to keep the pastors bland. Have the pastors give their sermons from their own experiences. They should never ask for the Enemy's help or, more importantly, invoke the Enemy's Spirit to speak through them to those present. Hopefully, the sermon will not be based upon the Enemy's word in the Bible. Try to assure that the pastors will close the Bible after the testament reading and before their sermons start. The Enemy's words are usually not referred to when the Bible is closed. Remember, most pastors don't dwell upon the words of the Enemy, they just prepare sermons. You should avoid like a plague pastors that have sermons that end with altar calls!

The collection plate—what a wonderful piece of brass it is! This is the focus of most pastors' sermons and is a crucial player in our war against the Enemy. Have many pastors use it continually by multiple collections in the service. This will make the plate seem to be a homage to religious greed and materialism more than anything else. Strive to keep your patient from seeing that the collection plate is useful and serves a greater purpose.

Perhaps you can keep your patient in a large church so that it appears by the large number of people there that the church is worthwhile. Many people go to church so they can get lost in the crowd. Most large congregations produce nothing that the Enemy wants for your patient. We can capitalize on that!

Have your patient concentrate more upon the people present within the church than what the pastor is talking about. Remember that the church is not perfect, although many feel it is. This disparity is good for us. Only the Enemy says He is perfect, but we know that only Our Father Below truly is.

Try to get your patient to experience mediocre prayers. If the communication lines from your patient to the Enemy are damaged, your patient will soon rely on his own inept prayers. This is the same as not relying on anyone, including the Enemy. This way, even though communication lines may be in place, they will not be used.

In concluding, even though your patient is attempting to go towards the Enemy's house, by no stretch of the imagination is he heading anywhere at this point but towards our camp. We still have a long way to go, but the Enemy will not quietly wait by the sideline for this to happen. If the Enemy does win, you will pay. There is always a scapegoat.

Affectionately yours,

Your uncle,

Korizo

Letter Number Ten

My dear nephew Bieshorn,

From your last letter, you said that you were frustrated. Your patient was thinking again! He was starting to notice how the Enemy wants him to spend his money.

I think most patients want wealth. Not just financial security, mind you, but they want wealth to shame Solomon. This serves many purposes. Wealth shows superiority over others.

We have developed the theory that most patients do not want to struggle and they are tired of fighting. Wealth is their way out. There are many get-rich-quick schemes that we have developed over time. Lotteries are one of our most lucrative. The idea of getting something for nothing is one of the best devices that we have concocted. It is important to keep wealth and success just over the horizon and then push it slowly further and further away from the patient. The patient will sooner or later grasp at the straws. His eyes will only be focused on the future.

Most patients want security in the world and do not realize that there is no such thing. The only security, fortunately, is in Our Father Below. Your patient is afraid of poverty, as most people are. I am sure that your patient is not aware that the Enemy provides for him in all ways. It is important that your patient does not realize what the Enemy has given him, but only thinks about what the Enemy has not given him. If he realizes that the Enemy has given him the gifts of life, food, clothing, shelter, and laughter, he is lost to us.

When your patient thinks about wealth we should put the Enemy in the situation. Whisper in your patient's ears that the Enemy wants tithes in order to be wealthy, too. Your patient must never realize that he should be giving to the Enemy from joy and love, not from obligation.

Church bingo is another of our great devices. It turns the Enemy's house into a gambling den to make people think about wealth in the wrong way. Raffles and fund raisers can be easily perverted if we are aware of what we are doing. The Enemy's own home brings in patients and does our work for us!

I find it interesting that your patient wants wealth because he feels he "deserves" it. He does not realize that the Enemy punishes those He wants to and blesses those He wants to. The patient probably does not realize that the methods of the Enemy will always be a mystery to him. To us, also. We, on the other hand, can reveal our methods and motives to the patient should we wish to.

Your patient is bitter because he thinks wealth should be given to those who deserve it. He sees money being showered on those who do not deserve it. He sees wealthy people as vain, eccentric, non-philanthropic sieves who waste money. Lifestyles of these rich, and infamous, people further our cause for new recruits to Our Father Below's house. Why your patient wants to be a sterling example of wasteful extravagance when he does not even like this type of people is a mystery to me. It is the way that most patients think. Don't ask why! It's just the way it is.

Your patient does not see that money does not solve life's problems. Problems change but do not disappear with increased money. Although some patients may not have to worry about placing food on the table with more money, they now have to worry about business, security, and hoarding their money. They do not realize that they are opening up a whole new can of worms.

I see that you have still not taken my advice to send a mosquito or two at your patient. You don't know the joy I experience watching a patient squirm hearing the mosquito flutter erratically around him. I do so enjoy the incessant buzzing of the mosquito as it drops like a bomb toward its juicy target. I have spent many a year watching patients waving their arms at empty air in feeble attempts to squash the bug, only to wake up with welts covering their bodies from head to foot. When used properly these mosquitoes will have the patient thinking about them constantly to the point of concentrating on nothing else during the day. I would strongly recommend you use them.

My advice to you would be to mentally twist everything your patient wants. Turn his desires into something we can use; something luxuriatingly evil that will assure the patient's place with Our Father Below.

Affectionately yours,

Your uncle,

Korizo

Letter Number Eleven

My dear nephew Bieshorn,

I have read that your patient is now "totally in love" with his girlfriend. Why couldn't they have fallen "totally in lust" instead? I hate the term "in love." It sounds too pure and sweet for me. I thought you were keeping him busy at work. Who gave him time enough for love?

From the terms of your last letter, I have noticed that there is a healthy dose of lust between your patient and his girlfriend. This can be a good sign. Lust always fades in a few years. It does not last. What is left after lust vanishes is cold reality. The ideals disappear and, with it, hope. No, don't have him think about lust. Just let him enjoy it.

At this point in time, make the attraction between the two of them stronger so that they are drawn like moths to a flame. Try to get them to take advantage of each other for sexual reasons. Sex is only a sign of love, but does not replace intimacy between two people. The Enemy associates sex with caring and affection.

We have to make sex the goal and an end in itself. Then they will concentrate on the sexual act and not the reason for the act. This can be brought about by minimizing the time your patient and his girlfriend talk to each other. Make them unsure of what they are getting because of the lustful mixed messages going on inside their brains. This way, they will not get what they want. Have them exclude the Enemy in their love! Try to twist the Enemy's words in what little conversation they have. "Subservience" and "dominance" are wonderful biblical words. They will help knock the Enemy down from His heights and push your patient into our waiting tentacles. Because of your clever mixed messages, your patient's prayer time will decrease and his girlfriend's prayer time will decrease. Continue having them spend more time with each other and less time with the Enemy.

I see your patient and girlfriend have placed themselves in a position where they idealize each other. They will be on their best behavior and not rock the boat. They will waste time cleaning their apartments because it will please each other. Their time spent on personal hygiene will increase, thus decreasing their time with the Enemy.

Be certain, now, that you pervert their love. Coerce her to think that this relationship is her only chance to have children. Tell her that her own job is not important, but only mothering a child is. For him, nudge him to think that this may be the only opportunity to have someone he can care for. I am sure you can devise many more devious ways to distort their love.

I notice they don't pay attention to problems that may arise in the future. Good! Keep them unsure of their financial responsibilities and their long-term goals. Have them start planning their future using material objects. Have them focus upon purchasing a home or car. Even a smaller purchase like a washer and dryer will help them attain a more materialistic mindset.

In the meantime, try to make your patient more aware of his girlfriend's annoying habits. I hope you are cultivating these habits with care. In time, we can use this information if we need to get more serious. Have the patient remember and relive the pain and agony he has had from past relationships. That is always good for points and I would wager that your patient will resolve to never let himself be that weak and open again.

While the two are martyring themselves, they will hopefully keep a score sheet of their relationship. I can see them keeping track of the wrongs, hurts, and pains they have caused each other. There will be a glorious reckoning sooner or later. The kettle will boil over and then smother the flame. Remember, the martyrs of today will always turn out to be the divorcees of tomorrow.

This letter is brief as we've received word of a church becoming stronger in the Enemy's Spirit. We have to go put out the religious fire before it spreads out of control, like a church revival.

Affectionately yours,

Your uncle,

Korizo

Letter Number Twelve

My dear nephew Bieshorn,

Reading your last letter made me feel wonderfully cold inside. Hearing about our patient's problems gives me such joy! He seems to be tripping over his own ego. His perception of his "inherent" superiority is working well. This is very good news.

Lead him to consider superiority as the goal in and of itself. Have him seek materialistic superiority and never let him assume a "servant" mentality again. If he gets a true servant mentality, your work will become more difficult.

There are many ways for our patient to demonstrate superiority. In a material sense, items can be displayed indicating his refined taste. These include artwork, jewels, or collectable objects that our patient would have that others don't. Intelligence is an excellent way to show "superiority". Use this weapon well. Intelligence can develop arrogance that he can vividly display by passing judgment on others. Many people confuse arrogance with self-confidence. To help our patient feel the superiority that he desperately seeks, use your wiles! As I wrote earlier, never let our patient realize that he himself doesn't respect people who admire themselves. We have been working hard for millennia to discredit human excellence. Let us not waste any more time!

Now that our patient has a love life, he has something visible and tangible to fight for in a material world. Have our patient push himself to extremes. Make him strive for success, for himself and for his loved one. Have him forget about the Enemy. Especially, coerce our patient to forget about His Son, who sacrificed Himself on a cross for everyone. Our patient should never see the Son's face reflected in the people he looks at. Try, when you can, to keep him from reading those accursed Scriptures. They're much stronger than our lies. We will never win his soul if he is armed with that knowledge. Keep our patient using his head and not his heart. The more he uses knowledge without wisdom, the more mistakes he will make.

We're monitoring that possible revival outbreak. We feel it's under control. The young fiery members now argue with the burned-out elders and this is helping. We have gotten both sides to concentrate all their energies on who uses the church's kitchen, and not on the Enemy. You never know when things might get out of hand again. Keep up the good work on our patient.

Affectionately yours,

Your uncle,

Korizo

Letter Number Thirteen

My dear nephew Bieshorn,

I read in your last letter that your patient is not getting angry when people disappoint him. This shows a definite change from the encouraging aura of superiority your patient showed in your prior letter. You wrote that your patient continues to associate in church with people he previously would not have associated with during the week. This is a bad sign. Try to make actions like this noticeable to him. If we can show your patient acting deplorably in the midst of the Enemy's camp, or he notices similar actions by another Christian, this is always to our advantage. Try to have your patient see inconsiderate people in church. For example, show him parents who bring their crying children to church and disrupt the services. Instead of being considerate of others and walking out with the crying children, these parents sit there. This can be demonstrated vividly to your patient—very easily!

I am sure that the congregation is on the older side. They all are these days, aren't they? This makes the church appear like a waiting room for death. The church does not get the young ones these days. We do.

During services, use your wiles so that the people will not use Bibles or open them. They should make no effort at all in church. Camouflage any attempt to show a fellowship before or after the services. Assure no one shakes hands or says "good morning." If they do shake hands, make sure their hands are damp and clammy. No one should volunteer for anything. You will not need to spend much energy on this, as people seldom volunteer these days. If there is a group social, try to make sure everyone brings salads and no one brings a main dish to eat.

Try to make church members "rainy day" Christians. They should not show up if the weather is bad. Hopefully, your patient will notice that the church is overflowing to the point of irritating the regular members only on Christmas and Easter.

Let your patient see the expensive cars and clothing the church members possess while the church remains destitute. Have your patient notice affluent people putting one single dollar bill into the plate. Make him see entrenched members pass up the plate altogether. More important, try to get Christians to intellectualize the Gospel. The Brownes and Thoumpsons in the congregation should do their best to make sure that the church is an intellectual church. These dry academicians will induce a good change in your patient, taking away all joy in the Enemy. Have them say things like "We'll pray for you" and then forget all about it by next week.

The Enemy is stronger than any denomination and surpasses their petty differences by His presence. Never treat the Enemy lightly! The Enemy is everywhere, and occasionally is trickier than us. He uses us at times to accomplish His wishes for His glory. I'm sure He learned this tactic of using others from us.

You have much to work on.

I have ordered my secretary, Snaiglime, to send you the proceedings of our actions on that possible church revival. Plagiarize any of our actions and conclusions for your benefit.

Affectionately yours,

Your uncle,

Korizo

Tempting Letters

Letter Number Fourteen

My dear nephew Bieshorn,

I wanted to discuss with you the possibility of making the patient itch more for success. This might help in the long run to get him to our side quicker, then into our camp, and upon our tables. The patient wants success materialistically but is not willing to work hard for it. He has been buying lottery tickets and sending for mail order "get-rich-quick" schemes. This is good! Keep him on the right path!

I see that he still seeks "stuff." Just the sound of the word "stuff" still rolls off my tongues. The more the patient fights for success the more we should make him spin his wheels. Because of his stagnation, he'll think that the Enemy's presence is not there in the workplace and become frustrated. We should slowly move him towards the realization that success only comes if it is placed above all spiritual ideals.

We should try to polarize everything. If he is not a success then he is a failure. We should not have the patient look back with the gift of hindsight. We should only let him realize how far in life he has to go. He does not realize that success, in the Enemy's definition, occurs when the patient yields his life to the Enemy. Nor does the patient realize that he has to have the Enemy's support to hurdle any obstacles.

It is good that the patient currently is not asking for help from the Enemy. But it is obvious that he is still wasting prayer time. His motives are wrong, praise Our Father Below. With time, he will become more bitter and cynical when his prayers go unanswered. It is wonderful to see Enemy soldiers fighting themselves for our worthy cause.

The patient does not remember the natural law of undulation. There are times of highs and lows in life. Surprisingly, the Enemy is usually seen and felt at the low times.

I was disappointed that you neglected writing me recently. Remember that the first law of manners here in Hell is reciprocity. You scratch my back and I'll scratch yours. Do not forget our devilish nature!

Affectionately yours,

Your uncle,

Korizo

Letter Number Fifteen

My dear nephew Bieshorn,

I read about your latest escapades with our patient. What a wonderful letter! It was a combination of efforts that shows you have been very productive. Congratulations!

Although you are close, you have not yet achieved what you are after. Having our patient fired from his job, being accused of theft, causing a car accident, fighting with his girlfriend, and an old girlfriend who phoned to get together again, has been beautifully executed. And our patient did not seek the Enemy while this was going on. At last our patient is learning to behave in a productive manner!

Our patient does not realize that everyone has unforgettably horrible days. We have to be careful, though. If our patient ever hears the Enemy's voice on Sunday, he could move back toward the Enemy's side. Our Father Below forbids it! There might be a reading that week from the Book of Job (who also had everything taken away from him). It is desirable for our patient to throw in the towel and send himself hurling onto Our Father Below's pitchfork while cursing the Enemy above. Our patient does not realize that the Enemy may be using us to try him. If our patient perseveres it leads to endurance and hope. We should be wary and continually watch our backs and tails for signs of the Enemy's presence.

Our patient does not realize that any break from fighting and struggling is normal. We know that when he stops to catch his breath, it is not easy to start struggling again. When he gives up all fighting and does not depend on the Enemy for guidance, he is ours. See if you can get him to drink some alcohol and possibly take drugs to get over this cascade of events. Our patient is not aware that the Enemy will not leave or desert him and that is to our advantage. Try to keep any real friends far from him and have only the pretentious ones nearby. Let him feel that he is being discriminated against. Our patient will eventually realize that hope is only for fools. Never forget—results are the only way we judge the future. A word to the wise is sufficient.

Let our patient dwell in his despair about the best way to commit suicide. Guns are always the best for us. Many of our patients prefer pills. Try every way you can to isolate our patient. In his misery, he will do our work for us. Have him call one of those suicide hot lines. Make sure the line is busy during the times he calls. Better yet, have them put him on hold, then hang up on him in the process.

Depression and misery are cyclical sicknesses that feed upon themselves. When our patient concentrates on his depression, it will get worse. There is always good and bad in everything. Our Father Below has his hands in all that is going on. Once again, good work! Keep it up!

Oh, by the way, I do intend to freely use your results for a talk I'm giving to an advanced tempting class on how I would prepare "Cascading Crippling Catastrophes."

Your affectionate uncle,

Korizo

Tempting Letters

Letter Number Sixteen

My dear nephew Bieshorn,

I was amazed to read your last letter. How depressing! Your patient just escaped entering our world by suicide. I can't believe he decided to go to bed early. Things always look better in the morning. You were so close. It was bad enough that our patient was found innocent of the theft charges and reinstated at work. But, to find out that he and his girlfriend made up was very bad news indeed!

I have given considerable thought to the best approach for your patient at this time. We have to confuse your patient. We must keep him busy and have life "noisy." This will keep him jumpy and unsure. We should never lead him to the only solid ground and footing there is, i.e., that of the Enemy. In the fold of the Enemy, all of our efforts are thwarted and deflected. What is worse is that your patient sees the Enemy's perspective there.

We should never let your patient walk away from our shining palaces built upon sand. Keep him away from those boring old houses of the Enemy built on solid ground. Try to convince your patient that the Enemy is in cahoots with us. Blur the differences between us.

Why does your patient wear blinders? He seems to be heading straight to the Enemy! Because every time we lead him astray, he finds his way back to the Enemy like a homing pigeon to its roost. This cannot be our doing. It is possible that we have overplayed our hand and your patient sees our handiwork. I believe your patient "knows" what the Enemy wants him to do. If we are partially effective, patients do not think about the Enemy until their old age. By then it is usually too late. Your patient "seems" to know why he is here. We have to work fast! Dazzle and blind him. Spin him about. Turn the world upside down. Make everything a carnival, event, or adventure. We want your patient to see with his eyes and not with his soul.

Remember, your patient must shut out the world to concentrate on the Enemy. Keep his mind busy during the sermons so that he will not patiently wait for the Enemy to give him spiritual food. Appeal to his sense of sight instead. There is much to look at in church. Be creative!

I noticed that you still haven't used one of the crawling members of the insect family yet. The weather is perfect for them. Consider them as a valuable tool in your tempting repertoire. Even if you do not feel comfortable using them, I think it would be wise to use a bee or a wasp instead of mosquito. They sting a lot worse. If you are fortunate it is possible that your patient is exquisitely allergic to bee stings. Let us hope so. Even if he isn't, bees do provide hours of amusement for your patient and will divert him from weightier matters.

Disturb your patient's concentration while he studies the Bible. Make him think about anything but the Enemy. This will disturb his effectiveness of his prayers. Overwork your patient's mind so that he thinks about more things than he can process. However, our investigations have indicated that the Enemy knows all the prayers of your patients in one form or another. He knows what your patient is trying to say when he prays no matter how he says the prayers.

I will let you know if I think of anything more.

Affectionately yours,

Your uncle,

Korizo

Tempting Letters

Letter Number Seventeen

My dear nephew Bieshorn,

I was pleased to find out from your last letter that our patient's friends are self centered and not Enemy centered. This is good. I see that he is still playing baseball once a week with them. What is their name? The Roving Marauders? That sounds like a perfectly good and upstanding Christian name to me.

Our patient needs the companionship of his "friends." He feels that not many people are close to him. Our patient is obviously very lonely indeed. He certainly does not have the fellowship of close Christians, prayer partners, or people that he is accountable to. See to it this dependency will never develop. It's encouraging that our patient finds Christians boring. They may seem so because the Enemy gives them limits and rules He wants them to obey.

It is good to see that his "friends" talk about drugs and bureaucracy. They seek their own individuality by fighting the system they are in and breaking laws. These people substitute good feelings from taking drugs for true love freely given by the Enemy.

I would avoid at all costs any signs of physical violence while our patient is with his "friends." If our patient sees our hand directly involved at this point, we will lose him. Keep him at ease with his acquaintances. He will not realize that he could be doing something useful for the Enemy in the time he is wasting with them.

I was pleased to see that the team was having a losing year. Convince him that winning is more important than the companionship he gets from these pitiful people. These people are devoid of the Enemy's touch and are already fully entrenched in our camp. Remember, as in the game of baseball, the object is to keep our patient from reaching the Enemy's home base at all costs.

I was very pleased to find our patient is happier with some alcohol in him. A drink or two to loosen him up is a good idea. Perhaps in time our patient may be encouraged to turn into an alcoholic. Let us work towards that goal. I am also pleased to see that our patient likes to see his peers lose their inhibitions with alcohol. I was also very pleased, but not surprised, to find that our patient finds pub life exciting. I am glad to see that our patient still likes dirty jokes and stays good buddies with his roving "friends." See if you can keep him coming back to our "services" at the pub in the future. Isn't it amazing how our patient walks casually from the Enemy's church right into our church?

Things look good right now. You have much to work on and I expect to hear great things from you in the future.

This is another brief note. There is a minor demon who is slightly annoying me. He is lecturing shortly on "Excelling Excellent Excesses" and I want to be present at the beginning to assure that he never forgets his hierarchical place.

Affectionately yours,

Your uncle,

Korizo

Tempting Letters

Letter Number Eighteen

My dear nephew Bieshorn,

No, I was not very frustrated when I found out in your last letter that your patient and his girlfriend were more in love than ever before now that they were back together. This reunion is a pity to me. Your patient and girlfriend seem to secrete an aroma of the Enemy when they are together. How can you stand to be in the same room with that stench?

I was pleased to read that your patient's debts are still high. Your patient obviously does not want to wait for the "good" life. Well, who does? He should buy whatever strikes his fancy. It is obvious that your patient is trying to regain lost childhood joys. We should let your patient indulge himself. Let him go crazy making payments for his indulgences.

Being in debt shows strong character flaws. His gluttony, greed, envy, and impatience should be cultivated further. You've been very negligent in developing these admirable characteristics. When these monetary ills seem worse to your patient, dangle a new bauble in front of him. Your patient will respond like a trained dog.

Time will lead your patient slowly to our lower spheres. The fact that he owes the next five years of his life to the bank and credit card companies works in our favor. I want to ask you to increase the pressure quietly and insidiously on your patient. Use our most skilled agents: The salesmen. Just the name "salesman" is as wonderful to my ear as is a briar under a patient's tongue. Many salesmen have already sold themselves to us and are very much like us. If they do not sell they do not eat. They don't believe that the Enemy will provide for their needs. These people lack integrity. They do almost all of our work for Our Father Below without our exerting any energy for the effort. I do so love salesmen!

Make them use their wiles to sell your patient something he does not want and will not use. Have them charge him a ridiculously high price for it, too! This will add another weight on your patient's heavily burdened shoulders. If you look at this on a larger scale, his debt diminishes his ability to tithe!

It is clearly not the Enemy's will that your patient gamble to increase his income. Give your patient unexpected financial pitfalls. Have his car die. Make him sick so he has to pay a doctor bill. Another approach we could try is to have your patient buy gifts for his girlfriend to show how much he cares. Shining little baubles are usually very expensive. This will increase his debt much more. I can imagine his inner struggle. His heart says, "buy something expensive," while his mind says, "buy something small."

Try to avoid having your patient and his girlfriend talk about their financial status. I am sure that he avoids the issue whenever he can. He is defensive because he knows the situation is not good. These are the times he will get angry at himself. This is a good thing. He will become depressed when he sees the predicament that he is in and then we can grab him.

In reviewing your past letters with some of the eternal high command, I see that we are slowly losing ground to the Enemy. This has to change! Remember that!!

Not very affectionately yours,

Your uncle,

Korizo

Tempting Letters

Letter Number Nineteen

My dear nephew Bieshorn,

I'm sure you have noticed that as your patient slowly heads towards the Enemy, he is starting to a feel a new sensation. This is guilt. Your patient feels that he is a failure in the eyes of the Enemy. He is. He assumes the Enemy's wrath is much worse than the Enemy's love. It is. He perceives that he has failed in the Enemy's eyes and he is afraid to face the Enemy. Consequently, he is running away from the Enemy. This is very good for us if we play our cards right.

Your patient does not realize that there isn't any way he can redeem himself by his own actions. Your patient knows that the Enemy is omniscient and this is why he feels guilt. As you know, guilt is a creation of the Enemy. It keeps your patient moving back towards the Enemy like a leash. Guilt keeps the fleshy beast attached to the owner.

We still do not understand how it could be that by the grace of the Enemy He cares for and loves unreservedly these worthless bipeds. Most patients give up, but your patient is probably overcompensating for the Enemy's love. He knows that he does not measure up and your patient should realize that there is no need to prove himself. The Enemy loves him regardless of his flaws.

Make your patient dwell on guilty thoughts. Make him think about future sins he might commit. Or, cause your patient to dwell upon past sins, which encourages guilt. This will ultimately have him heading back in the proper direction. Straight down!

Sometimes, your patient feels guilt and not love. Other times he feels love and not guilt. The times he feels love and not guilt may be the times he is most vulnerable. We should remember that patients constantly fluctuate. A momentary fluctuation in our direction does not mean that a patient will be caught and chained. If you cannot make your patient reverse his course, try to immobilize him from moving forward. Sooner or later your patient will stagnate. Then he will be ours.

Rub your patient's nose in examples of defiance against the Enemy. Show him others who defied the Enemy in the Scriptures and won. I hope he isn't still reading the Bible. I know he isn't if you've been doing your tempting properly. Make your patient aware that he has wronged the Enemy woefully in his life. Convince your patient that there is no such thing as forgiveness. Make him feel that his wrongs against the Enemy are with him for the rest of his life.

Once your patient realizes that there is no way he can follow the Enemy properly, he will give up. That is when we will prepare the banquet spit for our feast.

I would like to see if you can use some of those worthless baseball friends to turn your sheep back in the proper direction towards us. Try other efforts if you wish, but try something quickly!

Your somewhat affectionate uncle,

Korizo

Tempting Letters

Letter Number Twenty

My dear nephew Bieshorn,

I was further disappointed to learn from the eternal police that your patient is trying to teach himself patience. He is apparently learning the Enemy's will. You should have included that in your progress reports to me. You will be told of the judgment and punishment against you by the eternal high command shortly.

Never give your patient what he wants! You must act now!! His trait of endurance is quite annoying and must be drawn out of him. The rug should be yanked out from under him when he is within moments of grasping the prize he wishes. This must be developed dramatically to an art form.

Your patient will keep all his problems in front of him for years. Show him that people are moving in one direction or another. This will make him impatient because he is not moving at all, which will cost him his endurance. Make him lose patience with his friends and especially his girlfriend. As long as the victory is ours, I will remain patient. Skirmishes are just moves on a game board, nothing more. Winning is the only thing that matters. If you are not making your patient move ahead, make him feel like he is in neutral. Keep him impatient. Remember to let little things bother him.

I can understand your hesitation to use the tempting trick of the mosquito for many reasons. If you are unsure, you might want to consider another avenue. There is another insect, the flea, that you could use. This little bedbug has been happily chewing the feet and ankles of humans for millennia. It is very effective when applied correctly. Those four-legged enthusiastic canine or feline pets are portable flea hotels. Let your patient get close to these pets. The fleas will naturally sense the plump, blood ball delicacy that your patient is. Consider that in your attack plan for your patient.

Our advantage is that your patient's own vain interests and efforts are what he wants to achieve. The more the Enemy delays giving your patient what he wants, the closer your patient moves towards our fires. Your patient does not realize he could ask for everything he wants in the name of the Enemy. The peace of the Enemy will then naturally overcome him. He should not realize that this easy answer to his goals or desires will always be there.

I am sure that by now, if you are doing even a fraction of your tempting properly, your patient feels frustrated every time he looks in the mirror when he shaves. He sees the face of failure in front of him. This should make him very itchy and impatient.

Itchiness is a wonderful thing. Scratching never makes the itch go away. I intuitively feel, however, that you are in danger of losing your patient. The eternal high command and I demand you do better. Idle threats are never effective. You know exactly what is in store for you if you do fail.

Not affectionate right now,

Your uncle,

Korizo

Tempting Letters

Letter Number Twenty-one

My dear nephew Bieshorn,

Somehow, I knew it was coming! I just knew it! I was pleased, however, to read that your patient was having a difficult time proposing to his girlfriend. It must have been a pretty important week. Your patient promised to tithe better and propose to his girlfriend in the same week. As your letter stated with despair, she accepted, graciously. We are still investigating to find out what you did wrong. Considering your patient was not moving in any direction lately, he stepped forward recently with quite a large stride!

I could just envision this despicable proposal. They must have gone out to a quaint, but hopefully, over-expensive restaurant. I could picture him saying those awful words, "I love you", and "I'll love you forever." Then, he must have taken out a small ring and proposed.

Most patients do not realize that the size or appearance of the engagement ring is not important. I am very disappointed that your patient did not pay twelve percent of his yearly gross wages for the ring. We have been trying to instill that ridiculously high percentage into the minds of the populace in recent years. Try to get your patient and his newly engaged girlfriend to have a large wedding. This might compensate for the lack of money he spent on the ring, thus going further in debt. The first few years of wedded life will make or break their love. Lust will die during that time. I can effortlessly foresee some miserable times in store. We will have much fertilizer to work with.

Although your patient has proposed, let's see if you can at least do something productive about the tithing. We know the Enemy wants 10 percent of what your patient has. The Enemy says He officially owns everything of your patient's. We should have those nice baseball "friends" of your patient try to convince your patient that the Enemy does not need or want any money.

We should arrange that your patient does not tithe the way he is currently doing, with joy. Depressing, isn't it? I am very deeply disturbed to find out that your patient is giving happily. He realizes that his faith is being tested whenever he works at giving the Enemy his funds. Make him feel a pinch to give ten percent of his gross earnings instead of his net. It is good to see that your patient still has his pride. He still tries to make sure that others see how much he is putting in the collection plate. He should realize that what he gives with one hand should not be seen by others. Only the Enemy needs to know it. I am pleased to see that he still gets angry when he sees people that do not put anything in the collection plate.

We should try to make special callings at church for funds beyond the normal giving. Natural disasters are good excuses and so are special offerings. This will make your patient squirm when the plate is passed again. Remember that we want to play the fish as much as possible before landing him. Aggravate the situation whenever possible. Don't forget to use one of those boring pastors when you can.

I am glad to see that our patient still is having problems managing his funds. He is still trying to do it on his own without consulting the Enemy. I am pleased that you were very clever in giving him a small windfall. I noticed he did not tithe a penny of it to the Enemy. This is wonderful to exacerbate his guilty feelings. I am proud to see that you are working with what you have. It is good to see you on the right track again, even with the error of that proposal. Keep working, for we are watching.

Affectionately yours once again,

Your uncle,

Korizo

Tempting Letters

Letter Number Twenty-two

My dear nephew Bieshorn,

I found your last letter distressing. You mentioned that your patient was starting to give up on the credibility of science. This is horrible! Science is one of the greatest weapons that we have devised. What a friend we have in science! Science changes its opinion from moment to moment. The Enemy unfortunately doesn't change. He is boringly consistent.

For most patients, science is moving so fast that they play "technical" catch-up. Consequently, they are always watching science with much more interest than they are the Enemy. It is good that your patient has to keep up on scientific changes in the field. Anything that preoccupies his time and keeps his mind off the Enemy is to our benefit. More and more emphasis these days is being placed on science. We have to shake your patient's credibility in the Enemy any way we can. Use scientific distractions of any type to keep his mind from dwelling on the Enemy.

Humans have "devolved," if I may use the term, to the point where science is concentrating on the minuteness of the Enemy's actions. Patients these days do not see, or do not want to see the heavenly hand operating around them.

To clarify further, more effort is being spent on determining what the Enemy's work is, than listening to the Enemy.

Science tries to force the Enemy down to human levels. This is impossible. Most patients do not realize that science is incredibly limited and incapable of even partially explaining the Enemy and his works. We admittedly are having difficulty explaining the Enemy's works also. But our scientists are working on this challenge all the time and we hope to have this mystery unraveled shortly.

Many patients throughout the world share the opinion that if something cannot be proven in a laboratory, then it does not exist. Of course, they do not have the insight that we have. The Enemy's work and mind are too great for these lumps of flesh to understand.

We have "devolved" scientific thought so that the concept of the Enemy cannot be included. Humans, like your patient and the others, did that for us. They are down here below enjoying their just deserts.

It is amazing that the Enemy gave knowledge to these human fools without wisdom. With the aid of science, we now have the Enemy relegated to dusty tombs with other outdated philosophers. Remember from your schooling that "A" is for antiquated, like Aquinas, Aristotle and Augustine. Most patients never make their philosophical endeavors past the "A's" these days.

We should continue to devalue the Bible from a scientific viewpoint. We are having difficulties finding the smallest chink in the armor of the Bible and cannot dent it even using science. Many patients believe the Bible is erroneous in that it claims there were only six days of creation. If humans think about it rationally, six days of creation is at least as credible as evolution. Once a patient starts to believe that there are "problems" with the Scriptures, it is only a matter of time until they discredit them altogether.

We are pleased that most patients believe that miracles are not possible. They also believe that the Scriptures are invalid. Isn't it amusing how flimsy their faith is and how easily we can deflate it? Don't forget to use complex words like "infallible" or "inerrant" whenever possible. It is a simple task for even an inept tempter to make science as "dry" as religion. We just want our sheep to snack and graze contentedly all the way to the chopping block below.

Do not discredit this wonderful ally we have in science. It is one of the best ones we have produced yet. Use it judiciously.

Affectionately yours,

Your uncle,

Korizo

Letter Number Twenty-three

My dear nephew Bieshorn,

They what?!! Married?!! *AND YOU COULD NOT DO ANYTHING WRONG AT THE CEREMONY!!* Couldn't you delay the flowers, ruin the photographs, have miserable food, bad weather, have the priest demean women, lose the ring, have the husband sick from the bachelor party, or do all the miserable 10,001 things you learned that can be effortlessly done to ruin a marriage ceremony?

And they didn't go further into debt for the wedding? This is horrible news! I'll bet that even miserable birds were there in the trees singing beautifully, instead of ruining everyone's clothes at the ceremony like they're supposed to.

They got a bargain for the honeymoon? Really?! How could you?

Why couldn't you have them concerned with how much each person gave them for gifts? Or maybe have them concentrate on who did not share in the event with them? Is it asking too much of you to make them look at things on a dollar and cents basis instead of having people show up to share the "blessed day" with them?

I can understand your queasy feeling inside knowing that your patient and his wife went into this ill-fated marriage not expecting each other to change. This is almost an impossible situation for us to work with and puts you at a disadvantage to change them for the worse.

How could you write me such a miserable depressing letter? Me, your favorite uncle? It turns my stomachs. The letter only shows that your ineptness at such a simple little tempting has gone way out of proportion. If you could make your patient feel as badly as you make me feel reading this, I'd be proud of you.

I also read that they were not jealous of what they aren't. They do not expect to be perfect and have no regrets. No regrets? How can we work with that five years in the future when everything is routine and predictable? Think about that! And act upon your answers, quickly!

I see that they also found out that commitment is greater than sexual desire. If they adhere to this, you are in big trouble. Praise Our Father Below that both are still convinced that the other is still perfect. You still have something, albeit not much, to work with.

I would recommend burdening them with more children than they can comfortably support. Try to give the child some beautiful deformity if possible. Although it is not easy for us to interrupt with the birthing process, see what you can do about it. Maybe you will have some success soon because you have not had very much success so far. I would call you despicable but that would be praise to you.

One of the greatest weapons you have left to use is sex. This is the strongest force we have besides anger and hate to keep patients from concentrating on the Enemy. Have them concentrate on the feelings of sex and sex acts. Instill in them a concentration on the physical sensations instead of realizing that sex is only a sign of intimacy or means of conception. Try to make sex a sign of lust and desire instead of love. Yes, yes, I know you tried this with their sexual attraction in the past, but try again now that they are having sex! You are quickly running out of tricks.

I should not be totally negative concerning the wedding in your last letter. There are still some material crumbs that can be worked with. Small seeds were sown that can grow up to be big problems in the future. The bachelor party was a very good sign. It seems reminiscent to me of the heathen orgies from the good old days. This was very good. The groom got drunk and they had sexually enticing "strippers" appear. Now your patient cannot remember anything. That is excellent. I did notice that he is squirming whenever any of his other bachelor friends tell him about the things he did. It is encouraging news to see that the relatives on both sides do not care for the people that their children are married to. Relatives hating each other can be very good fertilizer for us to dig into in the future.

Things in general do not look good. You do not look good! At times I wonder why I take the effort to write! I am sorry, but the eternal police have been notified again of your miserable performance. You will hear from them, again.

Lacking affection,

Your uncle,

Korizo

Letter Number Twenty-four

My dear nephew Bieshorn,

I see from your latest letter that you took my words to heart. I am glad that the honeymoon had some nicely choreographed snags in it. She wanted to go slowly along the itinerary. He wanted to go fast through it, which created friction every minute of the honeymoon. I noticed that they had their first big squabble also. How nice. I am sure that they must have felt some second thoughts about things. Good work.

Magnify these "little" things out of proportion. We realize that the situation between them does not involve the Enemy very much and we can work with it. Give them different work schedules. Have each one start to assess the other critically and then assert themselves. Get rid of that heavy and bulky servant mentality they have. For example, if he says, "Let's go to a party," she should say, "How about a movie?" They'll hopefully end up staying home like sorry martyrs.

Each one is just beginning to sense that the other is not perfect. Capitalize on that, and keep repeating their trials. A temporary victory is always greatly diminished by a repetition of the trial. They have not realized that without the Enemy, they can do absolutely nothing. They do not realize that the Enemy relies on the trials in life. Although the Enemy stands firm, He believes in the theory of undulation. It is comforting to see that they are spiraling downward without the Enemy. They have been told by the Enemy to press forward with His help to obtain His goal. On the other hand, we will say anything they want to hear. Take this to heart! Lie to them and then give them nothing.

Our patient and his new spouse (which sounds wonderfully like louse, doesn't it?) do not realize that the Enemy can keep people waiting much of their lives if He wants. In the accursed Gospels, one patient suffered for decades while waiting for the Enemy to speak to him. Thirty-eight years of misery to be precise. And even though that patient escaped, that's what I call pretty good tempting by the demon. And, as all good stories end, the demon fully paid for the error of his ways for losing his patient. It's not the best ending possible, but it's also not the worst one conceivable.

The problem with these patients is that trials build perseverance and character. So, do not prolong their agony too long. Remember to change it. Try not to have them praying together. This can be devastating to us in the long run. For when two or three are gathered, the Son is present.

I am pleased to see that they have not yet discussed financial accountability to each other or to their new situation. How they spend their money can create very big problems for them in the future and success for us. It is nice to see new problems cropping up. They have difficulty in sharing the bathroom. This is proving quite an annoyance to them. They debate for hours on which way to roll the toilet paper! How amusing to hear them argue about their lack of quiet time! These little itches will grow into full pains before long and are very encouraging to see.

Now that our patient and his spouse are married, try to have them act as individuals. Remember above all, that divided we stand, and united we fall.

You still haven't used the flea idea I doled out to you, but good work on the honeymoon!

With a modicum of affection,

Your uncle,

Korizo

Tempting Letters

Letter Number Twenty-five

My dear nephew Bieshorn,

I read from your last letter that our patient was trying to spend time with the Enemy. However, his new commitments to his wife, his work and the little everyday chores decrease his time spent with the Enemy.

This is excellent news! We want him so busy that he will not have time for his morning devotional or his nightly Scriptural readings. It is our desire to have his prayers sandwiched while he is hard at work in the regimented office. This way, his prayers will always be quick and incomplete. This shows that his priority toward the Enemy is less than a greater priority towards the work force.

Make it noisy when he prays. Have an owl hoot in the morning. Make the neighbors in the apartment above him have a party! Construction on the street is always a noisy distraction. Have the neighbors fight, but not enough to make our patient move stronger towards the Enemy.

I would advise having things go very well for him now and remember always the law of undulation. Our patient typically does not rejoice with the Enemy. When our patient is having problems is the only time he gives credence to the Enemy. This makes the Enemy a "cosmic garbage collector," collecting garbage that not even He wants.

I clearly see from your writings that our patient is afraid at times to face the Enemy. He will even deliberately go against the Enemy's wishes, like a disobedient child, which leaves him weak and angry. He is ashamed of what he has done and is afraid to face the Enemy. He knows that there will be an accounting sooner or later of his deeds on earth, but not before he hangs himself.

Our patient typically will not praise the Enemy even with quick prayers. He does not recognize the Enemy for the creator the Enemy says that He is. Nor will our patient present his problems and goals before the Enemy in a meaningful way. Consequently, his prayers may not be answered. I am certain that our patient will not have time to spare from your tempting efforts to dedicate himself fully to the Enemy or the Enemy's causes. He will eventually renege on his promises to follow the Enemy and emulate Him and His Son. More importantly, note how our patient won't thank the Enemy for everything the Enemy has given him. This ungracious act will add to our balance sheet in later days.

In our patient's prayer life, have him talk very long and not listen. This way he will miss the most important part of the time spent with the Enemy. Being receptive to the Enemy's wishes, desires, and teachings is the most important aspect of prayer. With all these incongruities in our patient's prayer life, he will obviously try to convince himself that the answers he comes up with are the Enemy's answers. To me and my trained eye, your patient is predictable. He will rationalize prayer in every way he possibly can for his benefit. I see that encouraging response in everything else he does. When our patient is not receptive to the Enemy, he puts himself in the Enemy's position, usurping the Enemy.

We should try to convince our patient that his prayers will not "work" unless he sits in a certain position. This includes kneeling, eyes closed, hands together, head bent, or doing anything that will make it a ritual. Once this has formed in his mind, you can convince our patient that his prayers will not work unless he is at a certain location, i.e., at church. He will not realize that he could pray anywhere. He will think that the Enemy finds him acceptable only at certain places.

Every moment we keep our patient's mind off the Enemy is another second that distracts him and turns him toward Our Father Below. Our patient does not realize that he is expected to pray without ceasing. Once we get our patient to start limiting his prayer time, he will limit his prayer places and prayers in general. It is one slow step after another until he is in Our Father Below's home, burning for eternity.

Don't forget that prayers can be used to keep us away from our patient! They can cast us out and act as a barrier to protect him. I'm certain that you have had this happen. You cannot get through to our patient no matter what fiendish things you try. At this point we still cannot overcome this malignant power. How His power can be present in so weak a vessel as humans and be used by them is amazing! You would think that these meaty apes wouldn't even be able to access spiritual power, let alone use it! I am still surprised that their brains don't come out every time they sneeze!

Your affectionate uncle,

Korizo

Letter Number Twenty-six

My dear nephew Bieshorn,

In your last letter, you said that you were alarmed because your patient is moving away from materialism. The fact that he is moving toward a spiritual goal must mean that you are not using your tempting wiles correctly! It is almost impossible for the patient to lean toward spirituality on his own. I'm convinced your patient is trying harder to follow the Enemy. I would guess that even in his suffering, he is giving glory to the Enemy. The thought sickens me!

We must keep his eyes fixated upon material objects. This is totally opposite to the Enemy's goals. This will turn his face away from the Enemy. He cannot get away from materialism. See if you can make your patient substitute therapy for theology. Keep him subservient to the desires that exist in the material world. I know, this has been tried before in the past with this patient, but it has proven successful. Continue to make his eyes much bigger than his wallet. Have your patient not be bothered by beggars who ask for money. Make sure they do not use the words "please" or "thank you."

I hope the patient does NOT realize that sickness does not always disappear with faith and prayer. Many patients pray up a storm and nothing ever happens. Then, they'll get frustrated and possibly more receptive to our side. Sometimes, we can make people sick and sometimes not. Our scientists are still trying to figure this out. Nevertheless, we should try to disguise the workings of the Enemy whenever possible.

Your work is becoming more difficult. At this point, try not to have the patient deny the Scriptures he is basing his life upon. Twist the Scriptures ever so gently toward our ends. Don't make the patient aware that the Enemy uses pain or trials for a purpose. Make it so that the patient doesn't consider the source of his trial as either from the Enemy or from our hooves stirring up the dust in front of the patient's face.

The patient does not realize that the ONLY thing that matters is his spiritual life. Everything else is window dressing and food for us. Our patient appears to be content to sit grazing all the time. And, I am reluctant to say, he seems to worship the Enemy like a lamb led to the Enemy's slaughter. Unfortunately, worship time is the only time that he can finally put things in perspective.

Thankfully, most people only look at the world superficially. They use their sight, touch, taste, smell, but do not realize that they are not learning the things that are truly important to them. Try to make the patient do this. It may be possible to have him go in circles. Revive the issue of "sin" he thought long defeated.

Don't forget to dwell on my every word.

Affectionately yours,

Your uncle,

Korizo

Tempting Letters

Letter Number Twenty-seven

My dear nephew Bieshorn,

Isn't it wonderful how we place these funny creatures in a maze and watch then run around for our amusement? They believe they guide their own destiny. Even as we lead the blind further and further down toward Our Father Below, they still believe they have control.

Yes, from your last letter, I am sure that our patient was very happy once his new wife missed her period. Since then, they have found out she was not pregnant. It's too bad that we cannot tamper with human life all the time. Good effort, though.

On the question of abortion, these bipeds have the stupidity to ask if it is against what the Enemy wants. Of course it is! The Enemy gives the gift of life, humans don't. These creatures do not realize that each abortion is another notch in our gun belt one way or another. Praise to Our Father Below!

Try to make advocates of abortion. Make them believe that abortion is simple and painless. They do not realize that the unseen emotional scars are always worse than the physical ones. The Enemy has to deal with the free will of these creatures. After all, it was He who gave the freedom of choice to them. I certainly wouldn't have. Our patient has to give up everything to the Enemy, or not. It's all or nothing.

We should try to interject judgmental people into the abortion issue. People realize that they can sell newborns for quite a lot of money, which is admirable. There are parents who want children but who aren't able to have them. Abortion wonderfully warps one of the Enemy's greatest gifts and is almost a form of child abuse. Additionally, unseen emotional scars to the women will be left to fester, burn, and grow demonstrably in the long term. This will undoubtedly lead patients to Our Father Below, who awaits them with open talons.

Those who are against abortion use many rationales. Some say that abortion is murdering a living child and there are people who are ready to adopt. Others say that the world is not overpopulated and there is a joy of life that every being should be allowed to experience. All of these are fine and good, but Praise Our Father Below, most of them avoid consideration of the Enemy and what the Enemy's goal is in this.

Keep patients confused so that they do not seek the Enemy for guidance. They don't have to make peace with the Enemy. We just have to tell them to make peace with themselves. When they make peace only with themselves, they make peace with us.

Affectionately yours,

Your uncle,

Korizo

Tempting Letters

Letter Number Twenty-eight

My dear nephew Bieshorn,

I am glad to hear that our patient is being kept very busy. One of the foibles of being mortal is that mortals are always constrained by time. This leads to frustration because they know their time on earth is limited.

It is important that you do not give our patient rest. Keep him over-exerting himself. It is always best for our patients to rush with fatigue to Our Father Below. Coerce them to be tired and then give them a gentle shove in our direction. It always works out best when our patients do all the work.

It is best to keep him fixated on his goal. Just make sure that his goal is not following the Enemy. We want him to spend all of his time treading worldly water, and then, ever so slowly, go under. This will keep his mind off the Enemy as he sinks to Our Father Below. Have one of our "true" material goals just out of his grasp so that he strains towards it at all times.

The harder our patient works at attaining worldly victory, the easier it is for us to lead him to Our Father Below. Try to have our patient relive his past failures. Make him strive to accomplish something for recognition in a tangible sense instead of through the Enemy's eyes. Try to have our patient chase after his own tail. Give him problems too great for him to solve, but do not have him go to the Enemy for answers. Remember, the Enemy is capable of solving any problems that we throw in His direction, whether we like it or not.

Better yet, give our patient a goal and let him achieve it after much effort. Then turn the victory into defeat by making him aware that the goal he achieved was the wrong one. This is always wonderful to watch.

I'm sure you have noticed that my letters have been brief these last few months. And, although I'm not certain, I think I'm starting to repeat myself. Aside from the lame excuses one relative would make to another, the truth of the matter is, I'm convinced that you haven't been listening to my advice. I am tired of freely handing these pearls of wisdom down to you. They took long and hard centuries of experience to gather. You obviously cannot appreciate the fine advice I've dispensed to you. There must be a way that I can adequately charge you for these "jewels" I graciously hurl at your piggish feet. You must reassure me that it is worth my while to continue doing so.

Well, don't sit here reading my letter all day! Get back to work or else!!

Affectionately yours,

Your uncle,

Korizo

Tempting Letters

Letter Number Twenty-nine

My dear nephew Bieshorn,

I was very, very pleased to read that our patient is succumbing to temptations. It seems that you are on the right track once again. Such a lovely word, temptations. It just drools delightfully off the tongues as it is voiced. There are temptations enough to make our patient desert the Enemy and surrender to our side and Our Father Below. What is so wonderful is that temptations come in all sizes.

One of the most wonderful things about temptations is that they never disappear. We can shape them and call them many things, but still they are temptations. They have been invented and perfected through the many centuries of practice, thanks to Our Father Below!

There are countless temptations. There are temptations to eat ice cream, temptations to drive faster, and temptations to leave the Enemy. Whichever you choose, make sure it is insidious. Have him do it without thinking. Little temptations are wonderful! Tempt him to keep extra change given to him at the market, or gossip about other people. Pride and other such sins are wonderful too. You can use power, money, business, and sex to increase underlying desires.

Remember, we do not want overt temptations. We want them to slowly creep up and then overcome him. One of the best temptations to use is laziness. Get our patient to do nothing. There are many varied ways to use your tempting wiles to overcome our patient's upward momentum. Try to make him impatient once again. Then, during that period, idle hands will prove to be our lure and the bait for the hook. He will look for something in the world he can see and touch, then overcome his inertia by moving toward it.

For this patient, I would consider using the temptation of achieving perfection. Then show him that he is not perfect and that he cannot escape from making mistakes. What a wonderful temptation perfection is. Simply wonderful.

Pride could still be easily applied to this patient. Let him exalt himself. It has been steering him in circles since he first met the Enemy. He will not humble himself to anyone in the process. This, of course, includes the Enemy.

I don't think our patient is beyond using lustful temptations on, but with newlyweds, lust for someone else creeps under the surface. Lust for others will probably not reappear for years. File this away in your list of temptations to use in future days on our patient.

One important thing to remember is that temptations should never disappear. Have them repeat or change form, but never leave him without temptations. Temptations should be met individually by our patient and while he is fighting one, we can have others grow around him and entrap him. By the time he realizes what hit him, he cannot live without these temptations. Hopefully, our patient will not realize that temptations can lead him to the Enemy by seeking deliverance from evil. Once again, keep temptations insidious.

He does not realize that it is never the Enemy's plan to make temptations disappear. The Enemy wants our patient to involve Him in helping to cope with temptations. The Enemy wants our patient to willingly give up his freedom of will to the Enemy. To do this makes the Enemy a bigger fool than Our Father Below says He is. Why would the Enemy allow our patient to have something like freedom of will and then have the anguish and sacrifice of giving it up?

One thing that we should never forget is that the Enemy wants our patient to resist temptations daily. It is the gift of the Enemy that gives our patient the power to resist temptations. Not to totally remove temptations, but to resist them. The Enemy did not give permanent power to resist temptation. He knows as well as we do that our patients are totally self-centered. They would forget Him in time if He gave them that gift.

In one of their memorized sentences from that awful "Our Father" prayer, they ask for the Enemy to give them this strength daily to resist temptations and fight our ever-enticing evil. We should see if we could get someone to rewrite that sentence and the rest of the miserable stanza.

Good work. Keep it up. But remember, you have a long way to go.

Affectionately yours,

Your uncle,

Korizo

Letter Number Thirty

My dear nephew Bieshorn,

You are depressing me greatly! From your last letter it
is obvious that you have to keep your patient's mind off the
Enemy, at all costs! And you haven't been particularly
successful at all!! You must keep him from doing the
Enemy's work. Let me repeat myself. I would advise
keeping him overworked. Yes, push him even more than
you have been already doing. Have him work late. Have
him wake up early and make him too busy to act. Give him
much more commitments than his time will allow. We
want your patient burned out!

Once his prayer life falls, he is ours. Have him juggle
commitments and confuse his priorities. This will create
disorder with his family, his work, and then his play. He
will become ours totally, body, mind and soul.

These two-legged creatures are not very smart. Most of
them do not realize that they are going in six different
directions at once. They ask themselves why they are so
tired and why they don't get anything done. Most patients
are mad from being pressed for time commitments. For
your patient, you might have him pressured to make more
commitments by his wife, family or friends. You might even

try those baseball buddies of his. I don't think he has written them off yet.

Once he does make a commitment, try to make them useless ones. Parties with friends, sporting events on television, or washing his car are good time wasters. You also might want to place him at a sidewalk cafe watching people go by. Anything to keep his mind off the Enemy is a good thing. It chills my bones delightfully to see the world at an early Sunday morning brunch instead of going to church. Praise Our Father Below for bistros!

We should not let little distractions go by the wayside while we use bigger ones in deterring him to leave the narrow path he is on. Have his pen run out of ink. Or get gum on his shoes and blisters on his feet. Pimples on his cheeks would be delightfully good and anything that could irritate him should be used judiciously. It only takes a rock to make a giant stumble. A small pebble can also kill one. We lost one of our best operatives that way in the past. What was his name? Golleeth...Golgatha...something like that. We have learned much since them.

I would be so happy if you could do a little favor for me that will restore my faith in you. Get your patient to take off his wedding ring. That sounds like a simple request, doesn't it? A little twist is all it takes. It's off. Simple? You could do that for me, your favorite uncle, couldn't you? Not wearing a wedding ring tells the world that he's "available" and removes any sign of a covenant having taken place. It will attract others who cannot commit themselves and want to keep their options open.

I am still discouraged by the limited repertoire you use from your bag of tricks. Yes, I can understand your hesitation from grabbing the bee by its stinger, Bieshorn. Wasps and bees are too overt for you, it seems. Mosquitoes and fleas are too delicate and you lack the practice and dexterity to use them properly. I assume even making common house ants in his kitchen destroy his food is beyond you. I would like to remind you that even the common garden-variety housefly can still push him towards our cause. The fly doesn't have to be subtle and will annoy your patient to no end. It doesn't need much controlling and it can run right into your patient's forehead if you wish. But these techniques should be used now! You can hone your skills using your patient as a developmental tool.

On the other hand, it is nice to read from your letter that our patient is still having trouble communicating with his wife. It is normal, in married life, to give and take. Try to make the art of spousal communication a problem that he does not want to have to address.

From your letters, he is still facing problems without the Enemy's help. That is good. If he does not have the strength of the Enemy, his only recourse is running from the problems. Here is something insidious you can try. If you cannot distract your patient away from the Enemy's camp, you can distract him with time commitments in church. Have him join a men's choir, evangelism team, or have him become a Sunday School teacher. When used properly, these distractions will not lead him back toward the Enemy, which is a hazard we want to avoid.

Whenever I think about your patient, I see him slowly lifting each leather-shod foot, one after the other, towards the Enemy's camp. Do you? I would be frightened for you if he gets there. So, take action immediately!

Affectionately yours,

Your uncle,

Korizo

Letter Number Thirty-one

My dear nephew Bieshorn,

Your last letter alarmed me! How could you write me that your patient is trying to be a servant again! A servant!! Just the thought makes my fur stand on end. I thought we got rid of that problem. But, no! Now it seems to erupt like a ripe blister!! The hated Enemy has His power perfected in weakness. I can just see His cursed hand somewhere in this. I know it's there. If something is done in the service of the Enemy, your patient must give up power every time to do something for the Enemy. But the Enemy gives power back to your patient and more than enough to do the job. It is magnified and increased. Your patient, with the Enemy's help, has a will that cannot be defeated and holds a cup that cannot be emptied. Servanthood is the only way that gives true joy to your patient. We are almost lost!

Remember that the Enemy descended to your patient's level in order to serve human males and females by example. It is amazing to me that the Enemy does not understand the meaning of the word hierarchy. His world and universe is upside down.

Your patient realizes that it is always more important to listen than to speak. We have to consider that your patient will develop the thought that the individual being served is much more important than the individual who is serving. If he stays the way he is, he will become an image of what the Enemy wants him to be.

With news like this, I wonder if it is worth having you write to me further. Letters like your last one upset my sensitive digestion.

By the way, you should be receiving the bill for payment I am requesting of you for my advice and comments on your patient. High as it may seem, I would advise strongly to pay the fee for my services. The eternal high command would not be pleased to discover that you are not pursuing, with vigor, every possible avenue of temptation for your patient.

Without affection, but a payment might change that,

Your uncle,

Korizo

P.S. News like yours makes me hiss and can destroy my whole day. Do try to be more positive in the future.

Letter Number Thirty-two

My dear nephew Bieshorn,

I do not know how many times I need to state to you that it is not "healthy" for your patient to stay inside reading the Enemy's words and thinking the Enemy's thoughts. We have to get your patient outside and LOOKING for something exciting. For some patients, drugs, sex partners and other exciting desires work well. We have to have him look for something new, something different and something novel!! This lack of novelty pushes your patient closer to the Enemy. We have to convince him that he is stagnating.

The nature of human beings is that the human senses are sensitive to changes as well as stimuli. The Enemy says that He is the foundation and does not change. The Enemy tries to stress his consistency. This is the opposite of what we want your patient to think. That means that things cannot be constant.

We want your patient addicted to novelty. We want it so that novelty will wear off and he will have to search for new things. When novelty wears thin, he will hate his job, and sooner or later, divorce his wife. Make him search for new "thrills." Novelty is an admirable itch to possess and Our Father Below has formed it into one of our best conversion aids. Consistency will force your patient to look for different answers to the same old questions.

The Enemy designed humans to seek Him daily. He makes sure that all humans are left with a cavernous empty feeling that only the Enemy, or we, could fill. We must distort things so that your patient is constantly seeking something new in a material world. All patients, by design, must fill the ache that the Enemy created. All we want to do is to get your patient's mind off the Enemy. Is that too much to ask?

Your patient will naturally want to see something different. Well, there are movies coming out that are wonderful propaganda statements for our cause. These days very few movies tout the Enemy's rules. Praise Our Father Below, we have devolved art from creating something beautiful to making a statement. But do not have him see the beauty of the sunset, stars at night, or anything that even hints of the Enemy's handiwork. We have to avoid this.

We want to send him out on weekend evenings like everyone else, looking for something. We have to convince him that anything old is "ancient history" and not worth knowing. The furor with the Son was 2,000 years old and look how that has been dying out. Your patient is looking for the Enemy only in those places where the Enemy's influence is decreasing.

Novelty will keep your patient from ever turning his sights towards the Enemy. With the distraction of novelty in operation, your patient will always look outside of himself for the answers. The only problem we might have is if he turns his perspective inside.

I don't know what you have to do to jar your patient into action, but do it! Turn him into a gourmet insectivore! Try sticking him with a pin! I'd be overjoyed at any change in your patient for our good.

I still haven't received the first installment for my tempting consultation fee. No payment, no tempting advice letters! I will expend some miniscule amount of energy to script a brief letter to the authorities about how miserably you are doing against the Enemy. Remember, we are not charities (excuse the swearing) down here. Your installment would definitely put me in the proper mood to write more.

Affectionately yours (in a formal sense),

Your uncle,

Korizo

Tempting Letters

Letter Number Thirty-three

My dear nephew Bieshorn,

While the Enemy is at work and your patient is contemplating the Enemy, it is important for our goal, and our battle plan, that your patient keeps his mind oblivious to us.

When your patient does think of us, he usually thinks of us as spirits with tails, pointed ears and sharp teeth. He imagines anything that would make us appear ridiculous to him. He does not realize that evil is the lack of the Enemy's cursed presence. However, even here in hell, we cannot escape the Enemy's pervasiveness. Don't underestimate the Enemy! He is everywhere!

There are some pathetic examples of humankind who think they are smarter than Our Father Below. These people are truly wrong in their perception of themselves. Our Father Below, as you know, was an angel of the highest order. He was much higher and much wiser than humankind. However, he had a falling out, if you will, with the Enemy. It is almost impossible for humans to outsmart him or outthink him. The only way they can do anything against Our Father Below is with the help of the Enemy.

Praise Our Father Below that every time humans hear the word devil, they hear it coming from the mouth of a religious fanatic who threatens them with eternal damnation. This is a good concept to keep in their minds. This will keep people from thinking about and recognizing evil. You and I know that we do indeed exist. This letter proves it! People call Our Father Below the "adversary" and that is obviously true. He is against the Enemy, and He uses humans as pawns. There are so many tricks and ploys we use that the Enemy does not have much of a chance against us. Faith is so very easy to destroy. Love is so easy to pervert. Do you think it was difficult to make rose bushes have thorns? Our Father Below is unlimited in the universe and uses us to accomplish His evil goals. The Enemy is everywhere, but do not fall into the trap of thinking that the unseen Enemy is a powerless Enemy. We will yet overcome the Enemy and make the world ours. The victory has to be ours! It is all or nothing! ...I hope these inspirational messages stir you into action.

Oh, I was informed by our reliable gossip system Flybuzz, Gloopglorp, and others, that you have circumvented me and formally charged that I was extorting you concerning your patient. What a very droll effort on your part, indeed. Of course, I am extorting you. I proudly stand behind my record of extorting everyone without exception. Certainly, it is extortion between us officials in the eternal hierarchy that makes our system as effective and perfect as it is. Do not try in your meager way to change this again! The installment is past due. I await your payment eagerly.

Affectionately, for your accusations show admirable aggression,

Your uncle,

Korizo

Tempting Letters

Letter Number Thirty-four

My dear nephew Bieshorn,

I gather, from your letter, that it is apparent your patient is now acting differently. He acts as if the spiritual means are more important than the spiritual ends. This is devastating to our cause. In the material world, we lie, convincing all that the ends justify the means. It is the end result that is the only importance in the material world.

Let me refresh your memory regarding the fickleness of salvation. In the spiritual world, your patient does not realize that any patient could live an absolutely splendid life of worshiping Our Father Below. Moments before a patient's end, a patient can change their mind and move towards the Enemy's camp. If they truly believe that the Enemy's unending, all consuming love for the creatures forgives them, they end up going to heaven (excuse the cursing). In the spiritual realm, it is not important if the patient fails or succeeds in a task. It is the means that matter, not the ending. The only important thing is that they follow the Enemy and seek the Enemy's advice in their efforts. Once they surrender their problems to the Enemy, they can "rejoice" in trials and other pitfalls. They let the Enemy handle the means, thus assuring the end. We can make them stumble only a bit along their path but they will invariably stay on the straight and narrow. I would say this sounds like your patient, wouldn't you?

Try to be unscrupulous and slimy. This is the only way to win. Coerce the patient to concentrate more on the here and now. He should eat, drink and be merry. Your patient should never realize that the Enemy is adding a grain of sand on a balance scale for every thought and action of the patient. Whether the patient comes to us or not, the Enemy says He is the ultimate high court. However, you are ours and don't forget that! I expect great things. Your track record has not been good so far. Any second now it could be too late for you! If you lose your patient and things do not change, you are doomed.

Try to challenge your patient to make a public statement to the world about the Enemy. This usually intimidates patients and makes them squirm. Your patient may feel that others can flagrantly deny the will and rules of the Enemy if they want, not wanting to judge others. It is not "all right." It will never be "all right." Noncommitment ultimately shakes the patient's faith in the Enemy.

I am pleased that you finally sent me something! But there was no payment enclosed in the carton I received. It is unlikely that the contents were lost getting to me, but we are checking it out. Our inquisitors are beginning to coerce and subtly torture all who could possibly be involved in the delivery. I will keep in touch on the progress of this.

Affectionately yours,

Your uncle,

Korizo

Tempting Letters

Letter Number Thirty-five

My dear nephew Bieshorn,

I wanted to talk about the "same old thing." Such a sound, isn't it, "same old thing?" Even its name sounds musty and boring like a rusted antique. If you examine it closely, it has a faint echoing ring of defeat in it. If you listen very softly and look at people as they respond to it, you will notice most patients have a horrified expression on their faces at the mention of the "same old thing."

Have the patient focus on the same old thing time and time again. This way that he can glorify repetition to the form of a tradition. It will lose its meaning that way. Just like in the old schools where teachers use and abuse research. This abuse made the same old thing a wonderful tradition in academia as well as other places. This is wonderful for our cause.

Remember how the people in the desert tired of the same old thing for 40 years. They forgot the Enemy and the fact that the Enemy was blatantly taking care of them. I don't know how they could forget a pillar of fire, manna, and all that, but they did. This is not easy to repeat, these days. Try to make the same old thing obvious so that the patient can "predict" the actions of people. This may add to his pride. Remember the "same old thing" for us is victory and only victory.

The payment has arrived intact and is satisfactory. I am pleased with it. But you forgot to include the compounded interest with the late payment. Do not forget that once you fall behind in payments you are setting yourself up for significant penalties in the future.

Very affectionately yours (now that you have made payment),

Your uncle,

Korizo

Letter Number Thirty-six

My dear nephew Bieshorn,

That was a very clever touch of yours, when you made our patient react poorly to a problem. When that inconsiderate person cut in front of him in line, our patient naturally thought about revenge on the other person. Vengeance is wonderful. Let him simmer. Let him boil. Let the feeling fester. Let it itch and burn. Our patient knows that sooner or later there is an accountability factor and that the Enemy does promote trials and appoints afflictions, or allows them to happen. Our patient does not have to like trials, nor do we ever have to let those feelings of revenge against another disappear. Let his mind dwell upon them. Our patient is not willing to relinquish judgment and punishment to the Enemy. We can capitalize on this.

The Enemy says that vengeance belongs only to Him. Praise Our Father Below, our patient has not realized that the Enemy's timing is not his own. Our patient does not discern how idiotic he is. The Enemy and our workings are far beyond his peanut brain to comprehend. Our patient does not know that the Enemy can choose, for whatever reasons, to have a slime pit of a human being achieve success up until the day they die. They are then food for Our Father Below and they will reap what they sow.

Never have our patient question vengeance. He should not raise an eyebrow considering the arm for an arm, life for a life, even trade philosophy taught by the old school. Never have our patient perceive how incapable he is of judging. Isn't it gratifying how this insane human legal system many times has nothing to do with true justice? Human justice is blind because it can never glimpse the Enemy's hand in it and isn't based upon mercy. We can work with this. Try to get our patient to retaliate without seeking the Enemy's will over issues he feels strongly about. He will seek vengeance by himself, which is more effective and satisfying than giving it over to the Enemy.

The Enemy only has love as His main weapon. We, of course, can use anger and vengeance, which at times are much more powerful than love. We have to make our patient surpass the others so that he achieves little victories. These will add up with time. On a closing note, it is amazing how innovative patients get when they dwell upon vengeance. When they set their minds to vengeance, these patients are really like us in many ways and they would do us honor down here. It makes me glad. Maybe there is still hope for them in the future if they keep acting the way they do now.

This would be the perfect time and place to try to use a mosquito or a flea. It doesn't have to be a big one, or a mean one. Just pick one big enough to suck a little blood and leave a colorful welt in its wake. Think about it.

Affectionately yours,

Your uncle,

Korizo

Tempting Letters

Letter Number Thirty-nine

My dear nephew Bieshorn,

I don't know how you could stand to be in the same room with your patient when he tries to do unselfish acts. Your last letter to me said he was trying harder to emulate the Enemy. Blegh! This is a very bad move for your patient. I know he desires to place the Creator first, hoping peace of mind will arrive. I notice your patient finds joy in lifting up others' spirits and humbling himself. How repugnant. He even gave blood at the Red Cross last week. This is very disappointing. Blood is always best when given unwillingly. Your patient gets sicker everyday but not the type of sickness we would like to see.

You can try to corrupt his joy of pleasing others. Try the ploy of having others ask for donations. Or, make him believe he is "holier than thou," thus too spiritual for people to relate to him. Make him appear aloof and overly pious to others. Give him a "cause" that makes him narrow-minded. Then he'll become angry with others who don't believe or contribute to his causes. Develop this pride within him and the harvest you seek to reap with your scythe will be plentiful.

Praise Our Father Below that your patient does not have the hideous amount of patience the Enemy has. I see that he is still martyring himself for his wife. This is good. A storm is always lurking just behind the rainbow. The performance and actions of your patient have been absolutely odious to me, as has been your handling of him. The next thing you know, he will wrap a towel around himself and start preening his fellow beings by washing their feet. That will be all we need! Praise Our Father Below for the fact that people truly do not want to serve others. Their self love and self gratification is much stronger than their need to serve the Enemy.

I heard that his wife is expecting a child. Knowing the level of your performance so far, I probably don't even have to ask the implied questions about the parenthood of the child. The answer is probably blatantly clear. You disappoint me. This is just another example that you have not been making headway against your patient.

Part of the problem is the delay in paying me for my consulting services for your patient. Now that you are current in your account, I want you to review the letters I've written you to date. See if you have overlooked any tempting suggestions or methods that might prove beneficial against your patient. Your accusation that you never received my letters #37 and #38 is ludicrous. I would expect those excuses of a brand new trainee but not from a trained professional like yourself. Remember, as in the human legal system, ignorance is no excuse.

Review the letters. I expect better things soon.

Affectionately yours,

Your uncle,

Korizo

Tempting Letters

Letter Number Forty

My dear nephew Bieshorn,

No, it was not me that informed the eternal police that your patient was becoming more Christ-like. Heavens! I went and said the "C" word! I'm turning into a chancre sore. Now Snaiglime will have to write the rest of this for me. I have to wash my mouth out with soap to get rid of the disgusting taste that word leaves behind.

(There is a change in penmanship)

It seems, nevertheless, as I said, that your patient is becoming more "C"-like. Why would I inform the eternal police about you? You are my favorite nephew, aren't you? And you are current on your payments, aren't you? I'll check into this and see if your account is up to date.

Your patient seems to understand that suffering is a part of his Christian walk. This is a very bad revelation for your patient. Your patient is aware that he is totally undeserving of any grace or mercies by his very nature alone. He knows! Yes, I am sure of it. He knows! This makes his mind more difficult to corrupt.

Have your patient repent as some sort of reward system. He'll think that if he repents often enough, the Enemy will bless him. Many patients believe this to be true. Your patient is not aware that just the acknowledgment of repentance is moving towards that goal.

If your patient knows that he is imperfect to the Enemy but does not repent, the Enemy will not forgive him. The stones cry out as Our Father Below cackles and watches the slow descent of your patient toward the warmly repugnant bubbling ooze down here. If the above reference to the ooze made you homesick, you'll just have to suffer up there until your job is done.

While we are on the subject of repentance, the final report from the eternal police concerning your status is coming. I am sure that you are aware that we do not have repentance here below. Words like "I'm sorry" or "forgive me" are unknown here. If you do not have a leg to stand on, you will stand on no legs.

Affectionately yours,

Your uncle,

Korizo

P.S. Oozeblurgl, in accounting, just reported that your are indeed behind again in your payments. I do not care where you get the payment. Just get it!

Letter Number Forty-one

My dear nephew Bieshorn,

It has been a while since you've written. Yes, I am healthy once again and back to my own self, no thanks to you! I was surprised by your last letter. You were always good at whining, sniveling and whimpering. You say you are now at your rope's end, trying to tempt your patient to separate him from the Enemy. You did beg magnificently, pleading for any tricks left to try. I still have not yet received your payment, so I am sure you understand the brevity of this letter. I have dispensed my best nasty tempting tricks to you which you have shamelessly botched up. There are only a few left.

Thank Our Father Below for a trick I mentioned to you before, by the way, that we could use to our hearts' content: intestines and stomachs. All patients have them and we can use them in many sly ways. Let your patient's appetite lead him. Force him to waste time by eating long, expensive meals. Have him eat meals that cost a fortune and signify nothing to the Enemy.

It is wonderful to see people spending quality time in the kitchen instead of worshiping the Enemy. Try to turn your patient into a connoisseur. Have him know his wines. Make the meal his high point of the day so that it will supersede his communicating with his spouse. I know your patient wants to be meticulous so that he can concentrate his entire being on his preparations of this meal.

It is obvious that your patient could become seriously addicted to food, possibly more than to the Enemy. He is obviously not yet concentrating on eating and drinking as much as he is on the Enemy. If you cannot get him to consider food as a delicacy, then try to get him to consider food and drink as a luxury. Try to have him lose weight. Weight watching can be an obsession in itself. There are innumerable twists and nuances to the sin of addiction.

Food does not help the Enemy's Spirit instruct your patient to hear the Enemy's voice. Your patient doesn't realize he is less than a wisp of a mist that appears just for a short while and then disappears. If patients did, they would realize that they are wasting their time on superficial matters. This should help you out a little bit in finding a new route to tempt your patient from the Enemy's grasp. I know you are almost out of tricks, but now, so am I. This is a very bad situation indeed.

Affectionately yours,

Your uncle,

Korizo

Letter Number Forty-two

My dear nephew Bieshorn,

From your last letter, I see that your patient is still trying to do the will of the Enemy. We must remember, if your patient does not do the Enemy's will towards another person, the Enemy will say, "I'll do it myself." All patients operate under a time constraint. Praise Our Father Below, time is a concept we demons do not have to deal with. As you know, time is fleeting and marches on. The meter is ticking, urging your patient to seize the moment. This time constraint acts upon your patient constantly.

You might want to give him some worldly pursuits to waste time. Try to get your patient to do redundant things. Make your patient aware of time. Your patient will watch himself growing old. Most patients try to stop the aging effects of time with cosmetics. The more stubborn patients are, the harder they try to reverse time. They're the ones who are focused upon narcissism, and us. How can a patient hope to defeat the Enemy's concept that beauty is fleeting?

Human creatures always want to look back in time. All fleshy watersacks are the same. I can state, unequivocally, that they do not want to age. They want to reverse their age so they look young forever and not focus upon their future and towards death. Aging is the Enemy's way of telling your patient not to squander time. All patients have to meet the Enemy eventually face to face, and all of them are afraid of that. I have been told that we have to meet the Enemy one day also. Gulp! I am not afraid of the meeting, but I do pride myself on my ability to spout grandiose lies. However, remember that we do not want to give your patient time to accomplish His will and His goals.

There is a day of judgment for all of us. Humans avoid the issue. It is like the deadline for paying income taxes. They do not want to face it. They will avoid it with every ounce of strength they have. There is a bottom line to their life on earth. If they live a life separate from the Enemy, the Enemy may give them what they want–separation and solitary confinement. We think it is better for us to tell the humans not to approach the Enemy. But to work this for your patient, I would advise you to get some zealot to do the opposite; advertise the issue. A sign with the words "The End Is Near" will always be laughed at. Isn't it amazing how these prophets are always demeaned and degraded no matter when in history they arise?

I hope this helps you understand your patient a little bit better. I look forward to your next approach to changing your patient. Make haste, for I can sense the Enemy is about. Pass your paranoia along to your patient.

I did take the effort to review the best of my tempting tricks to use. It seems to me that insects are still among the best tricks for use on your patient. I order you to use them, instantly! If you don't, you will pay!

Very affectionately yours,

Your uncle,

Korizo

Tempting Letters

Letter Number Forty-three

My dear nephew Bieshorn,

I was surprised by your inactivity in the last few months regarding your patient's life. I know you are still having trouble figuring out which direction to take. Let me tell you a little bit more about your patient and what has happened to him.

It is impossible to be a servant without a master. Your patient has a master. Your patient is wearing a yoke. When following the Enemy, the yoke your patient wears is easy and light. Some people are never satisfied wearing any type of yoke. Consequently, they do not realize the trade off. If they invoke the Enemy to remove their yokes, it is a useless prayer.

I saw it coming! Yes, I did. Your patient has had a "shift" in consciousness. The Enemy did it again. The Enemy has set your patient free from lust, greed, and other vices that we manipulate with extreme art. Your patient has been given a purpose to himself. He now has perspective as to the mechanism behind creation and the universe around him.

Most importantly, your patient is free from death. Death is one of our greatest tools. He is free to face death without fear because he knows that death has been conquered by the Son. He knows what happens after he dies. There is the bitter transformation from oneself to the image of the Enemy. Your patient is free from depending upon his limited self. The world makes sense to him. He is free from asking questions about important matters in life. Your patient has been given answers: Who am I? Why am I here? What are these things happening to me, and why? All these questions have answers only when a patient is snuggled warmly in the Enemy's fold.

Your patient is still free to experience pain, suffering and misery. Your patient is free to fail, be abused, and martyred if need be. Your patient is free not to be perfect. Only one human ever was; curse the Son. Your patient is free now to rely on his meager endeavors. He can depend on his heart, which is trying to imitate the Enemy's. He is free from seeking revenge and he is free of worries about clothing, food, and material things. Your patient does not worry about tomorrow. He gives everything up to the Enemy and lets the Enemy do everything for him.

I leave it in your hands as to the next avenue you should pursue. That way, the blame is completely yours if you fail. I believe you have lost already, but I am willing to scavenge what I can from your mismanaged situation. Which reminds me, if you are having trouble making payments, let me know. I am sure that I can be creative in finding new ways to suck blood out of turnips.

Affectionately yours,

Your uncle,

Korizo

Tempting Letters

Letter Number Forty-four

My dear nephew Bieshorn,

Your absence in writing me or taking further action against your patient is alarming! It has been months since your last letter. You clearly must be at an impasse. I want to fill you in a little bit more on how the Enemy works. This will give you some insight to what makes your patient work.

The Enemy could easily make automatons out of these bipeds, but chooses not to. The Enemy really loves these beasts so much that He has given them freedom of will. It is surprising to us that He does not impose His cursed will on these creatures, but He doesn't. Our Father Below uses His power in exquisitely painful ways. How so much power could not be used properly by the Enemy is amazing to us? The Enemy does send His Spirit to your patient before your patient asks. He does love those who deny Him and even curse Him.

He expects patients to read thrice-cursed book, the Bible. There is no apparent supervision by the Enemy at times. There is no eternal police, no supervisor devils, no nothing. A patient is left to himself or herself. The Enemy wants your patient to follow Him by his own decision. The Enemy gives back with one hand what He took away with the other. After a while, the Enemy does not make His presence known to your patient as in the beginning. The Enemy still expects your patient to follow Him, nevertheless. He must have learned this from us. To our arithmetic, your patient is eventually left with nothing. This is also what we give him.

At times, the Enemy does test him, but not more than He knows he can take. He still expects your patient to follow Him during and after any testing he has had. He expects patients to stumble and try to follow Him in the best way they can. Some of these maneuvers are even laughable. That seems to be all the Enemy wants!

As crazy as it seems, the Enemy gives these stupid, cow-like creatures power and freedom of will to live their lives and do what they want in their work regarding the Enemy. I know that this does not make sense to you, for it has never made sense to me. That's the way it seems to be right now. That's what I have been told, anyway. I hope this information will help you, although I do not see how.

Affectionately yours,

Your uncle,

Korizo

P.S. Your payment is seriously past due. It is imperative that I be paid first before any of your other obligations are taken care of!

Tempting Letters

Letter Number Forty-five

Bieshorn,

From all the latest reports I have received from the eternal police, your patient is as good as lost. Perhaps that is why you haven't written in ages. I warned you. All this is your fault! Yours alone, not mine! I can fully document your errors and my exceptional behavior beyond reproach in this matter. When your patient's life is over, unless you can come up with a "miracle," he will rest with the Enemy and you will be the main course at our dinner.

Your patient is committed to the Enemy unconditionally. It is a certainty that your patient will never be down here with us. I would wager that he would rather smother himself than consider accepting our fine and considerate hospitality. I am sure that your patient sees the face of his Lord and everyone he meets with the Enemy's Son's message, "I died for you." Disgusting! I can just see the repulsive look on your patient's face showing all His love. How kind your patient must be! He's a regular saint! Yecch!! I am sure to my olfactory senses, he has become an odiously strong stench of the Enemy. I would hazard to guess that he even smiles at strangers. It is so revolting that words to describe this fail me.

He must have that horrible joy of knowing the Enemy and sharing a spiritual relationship with Him. I am equally sure that he is not supporting a fire and brimstone salvation. He is probably dealing with people and showing them that he is Christian by his love.

Even worse, I am sure that he wants for nothing. Nothing! He prays for the Enemy's will to be done. If this isn't a patient beyond our ability to influence, I will trade in my tail.

Perhaps the final straw is seeing that he is on the visitation committee of his church. How despicable! He's actively recruiting soldiers against our cause!! This sickens me and worries all of us down here with the petrifying thought of new soldiers in the Enemy's camp. All this news gives me a headache and upset stomachs. There is a bad taste in my mouths at the revolting thought of that.

Let me tell you about your victor. The Enemy loves anyone unconditionally from the first breath to their last. This Enemy pours out his love much more than any patient is worth. We don't know why! He just does! Your patient could spit on the Enemy and the Enemy would take your patient back in an instant. This has been seen and documented by us in the past. We know that it is true. Perhaps the reason your patient is now beyond our grasp ultimately is that he is rejoicing in everything.

This rejoicing will not always apply to the child he and his wife just had. I am truly horrified and appalled that the child turned out beautiful in every way. Praise Our Father Below, there are at least two times where the child may still prove useful to us. One is the terrible two's, where the child will be two years old, screaming over everything and trying the patience of everyone. This can possibly turn things to our advantage. Once again, don't expect a "miracle." There are no such things. The second time where a child is helpful to our cause is when the child is in the terrible teens. When children seek their independence, they will usually rally to our causes. I like teen-agers! They are usually miserable to everyone because of their growing pains.

A new tempter has been assigned to the child and to your patient. We know that you are not good at your official job. As of now, you are relieved of duty, disgracefully.

I have the feeling that your patient at best is only a load of dust in a small apartment. This dust ball lives in a small city, in an insignificant country on a turning world. He exists in a miniscule solar system in a nondescript galaxy but listens to what the Creator tells him to do. This dust ball is loved and will end up happy and at peace. You, however, will not! This is not a good end for the dust ball, or you.

The eternal police have been notified to take you into custody. You will soon learn a new meaning to the word "hell." I hope that your fear may increase in the slow simmering interval before capture so that you will become tastier to us.

I assured you that I would be paid one way or another.

Not affectionately yours,

Korizo

P.S. Please don't write again. Your information turns my stomachs and makes me vomit. I disown you.